AN ENGAGED LEARNER: A POCKET RESOURCE FOR BUILDING COMMUNITY SKILLS

REBECCA NTHOGO LEKOKO

PARTRIDGE

A Penguin Random House Company

To order additional copies of this book, contact
Toll Free 800 101 2657 (Singapore)
Toll Free 1 800 81 7340 (Malaysia)
orders.singapore@partridgepublishing.com

www.partridgepublishing.com/singapore

CONTENTS

ACKNOWLEDGEMENTS

Many friends and colleagues have helped in shaping what gives this book its worth. Not least among them is the Dintoe's family, whom I had the pleasure to visit in St. John's Newfoundland/Labrador, Canada during the time of writing this book. Memorable are the times when Susan and I discussed about contents of this book anchored on our experiences as teachers and Mr. Dintoe did some editing, tapping from his years of experiences as a teacher too. I can't thank you less Kitso, memories of your kindness, the mouth-watering dishes, our quiet chats about this and that are deeply engraved in my mind. Thanks to the little ones, Sakhile and Oratile, who kept reminding me of great things that make up families; play, laughter and joyous noise that sometimes came at the right time of my mental block and would be happy to watch you jump around. When friends are mentioned, it would be a grave omission if I don't mention Dr. Constance Mugalla, my long time friend who always has a room for me in Atlanta, Georgia, USA whenever I want a quiet place to rest or do my work. Your ideas and prayers have helped in ways that words cannot succinctly capture. I want to thank all my friends for being supportive and kind to my feelings.

I was also privileged to have been welcomed to a Spring Institute (June 2011) on developing a teaching dossier at the Memorial University of Newfoundland, Canada. It came at a time when I was writing Part 3 of this book. The workshop played a key role in helping me refine and add to this section. I genuinely want to thank the presenter Allyson Hajek for her resourcefulness.

I am extremely grateful to the Trafford Publishing Singapore for making my dreams of publishing this book come true and for greatly enhancing the visual and other quality aspects of this book.

I want to give thanks to my family. If it weren't for them, I wouldn't have had the drive and energy to write this book. I know I make them proud to achieve something valuable like this one. Mphoentle, Kaone, Ikie and Yvette, I love you sons and daughter and I am glad you are there to give meaning to my life.

Finally, I dedicate this book to my late father, Mr. Moleki Lekoko who passed on when I just started the writing process and to my mother whose life for me is a torch to dignity; respect, appreciation, love, courage and determination. Without them, my eyes would never have been opened to the bright rays of the sun and known that 'you make hay while the sun still shines'.

Thank you all. Le ka moso!

PREFACE

In this book, I make a case for functional community skills. These are skills that will help learners to function beyond the four walls of the classrooms. My view is that every teacher, facilitator or trainer teaches these skills. Every time when we teach; when we give learning activities; discuss or attend to learners' questions as well as making certain conclusions, we are conveying a certain view about the worlds and people in them. Teaching community skills is all about making learners aware of these worlds in and outside the schools' environment and how people live in them. It advocates for creating "a better fit between what it takes to live in today's societies and what educational institutions provide" (Davis, 1993:10). We are reminded here of Dewey idea of education for a democratic society. He actually "warned that so long as we divorce school work from social values, we also divorce the intellectual from the moral, encouraging our students to be selfish when we ought to do all we can to support their natural instincts to serve and work with others" (Dewey cited in Kaplan, 2009:337).

Obviously, we learn because we want to apply what we learned to our social worlds, for example, world of work, world of family, world of citizens, world of religious, etc. This calls for a broader vision of learning that is situated in our "social, cultural, political and theological contexts" (Kincheloe, Slattery & Steinberg, 2000:45). That is, learning should be understood as a tool that ingrains values or skills of how to live in real worlds. Like Osborne (1991) says, we should see 'a classroom as a microcosmic society'. What should persuade us more to teach these functional skills is an understanding that "all students will eventually leave school and proceed with their lives as workers, citizens and members of a family" (Gardner, 1999: xi). Yes, learners do not stay forever in our classrooms. They are on transit and facilitators should support and facilitate their smooth transitions to these other worlds. It is for this reason that I am convinced that we have a social and principled obligation to ensure that functional community skills are developed.

To address the needs for functional skills, I make a request to all those who are predominately bookish in their teaching and learning to re-examine this type of education against the type of learning needed by individuals and communities to survive. Putting an emphasis on success as grades rather than acquisition of functional skills is shooting down our efforts and having no one but ourselves to blame if what we learn and teach find no place to be applied in real worlds of our living. The very reason that a person can intentionally plan his or her learning is the very same reason that he or she should be selective in what he or she learns or teaches. A sure way to ensure functionality is to let learners explore contents that closely resemble lives as lived in different contexts. Searle (1981) directly influences this position. He makes it clear that

> the school exists to create a symbiosis with the community outside it; it is a people's resources. It must move towards them, its students and teachers helping in agricultural production, the acquisition of literacy, the gathering of oral history, the formation of factory brigades, the cultural interchanges, the lending of students' developing scientific knowledge in the

construction and expansion of communal villages and communal suburbs (p. 4).

The ideology espoused here makes resources for learning abundant and available for everyone as no one is privileged at the expense of others because community resources are readily available. Most of these resources are free for all to use. In short, "the learner must learn about the environment in which he or she lives, the organization of the political and social structures of which he is a part [and] the pattern of local production" (Development Dialogue, 1978:75). When thinking about communities as resources for our learning, we must be reminded that the era in which we live is that of a 'global' village. This, as explained by Braman (1996), means that our social relations stretch across communities, making the locals and nationals to be interpenetrated by international forces. This type of global community gives learning its form, meaning and utility. The key principle is application of what has been learned across settings.

Facilitators have a critical role in the development of these community skills—to produce graduates with apposite levels of academic achievements and broad skills like ability to think, collaborate, be responsible, make decision, innovate, solve problems and relate well with others. Everyone, almost everyday use these skills, perhaps as a parent, worker, a community leader or just, simply, a citizen. To teach these skills, is to ensure that learning activities shape a future of possibilities and better living for all.

HOW THIS BOOK IS ORGANISED

Introduction

This book is organized in chapter-headings. However, this organization does not rule out the possibility of some necessary overlaps of contents and strategies. Notable is that much of the discussion on contents, learning/teaching strategies, processes and outcomes are tailored more towards adult learning contexts. Case studies that are presented also illustrate this focus. This direction is influenced by my experiences as an adult educator. However, educators and learners in different contexts will find this resource useful.

How the chapters are organized

The main chapters follow a similar pattern of

- An important quote shedding light on the main lesson or message of the chapter. The introductory chapters do not have these quotes.
- Introduction that makes readers anticipate or understand what the chapter covers.

- Case studies that mainly serve to illustrate how a certain skill can be taught or developed. Some introductory chapters do not have these cases. The cases form a foundation for discussing the importance of the skills being developed. In some instances, cases are used to illustrate ways in which what has been learned can be applied in real life encounters outside the classroom environments.
- Learning activities come in different forms, for example, games, quizzes, descriptive or narrative encounters. These are not uniformly presented in all chapters.
- Reflection questions come at the end of the chapter mainly to pose some broad questions to remind readers of the chapter's main lessons. The reflection part certainly does not mean that educators and learners cannot or should not come up with their own preferred learning activities. It is highly encouraged that readers innovate assessment exercises to suit their specific learning environments.

Chapter lineup

This book **'An engaged learner: A pocket resource for building community skills'** is organized by important topics directly relevant to building community skills. Sometimes, there are sub-topics to the main headings to capture specific emphasis about a particular broad topic.

Brief synopsis of the chapters

Chapter 1: Aims and Targets	This chapter outlines what the author sees as the reasons behind writing this book. The main goal is to make a case for community functional skills. Institutions

cannot exist without communities from which learners and facilitators come from. This mutual implication alone prevents learning institutions to close communities out of their missions. A number of authors are brought in to support the claims of the importance of community skills. The chapter also presents important principles guiding the discussing of these community skills. It concludes by defining the targets for or audience of this book.

Chapter 2: The Concept of an Engaged Learner

The concept of 'engaged' learner is explained and linked to related concepts of applied learning, active learning, purposeful learning and lifelong learning. This philosophy is explained especially as a pre-requisite to teaching community skills which requires that learners be actively involved in and outside the classroom walls. It makes a point that learning that concentrates on concepts, ideas and theories alone at the expense of application falls short of fully engaging learners. It ends by giving and explaining the characteristics of these learners.

Chapter 3: Context and Contents

This chapter presents two concepts of content and context that cannot be avoided when learning experiences are discussed. The concepts are described in relation to how they influence what goes on in the learning environment. A claim is made and explained about the relationship between contents and contents, for example, that, content exists as part of context. Case studies are brought in to illustrate the importance of including these as we plan and engage in the actual implementation. Moreover, the discussion of content and context are brought in to drive home an important point, that, we teach in heterogeneous contexts where people of diverse backgrounds coexist. Thus, we expect learning experiences to differ in different ways especially in content and context.

Chapter 4: Process and Outcome	This chapter discusses two important concepts of process and outcome. The two concepts are defined, then, cases are brought in to illustrate their critical position in the teaching-learning environments. The statement that says 'we engage in learning hoping to achieve something' demonstrates the indispensable connection between these two, the learning process (all that learners do to acquire some knowledge, skills and attitudes) and the learning outcome (what learners emerge with from the learning process, like knowledge, skills and some attitudes). The discussion is enhanced with relevant literature and case studies.

Chapter 5: Pedagogics of Thinking	A case is made for developing thinking skills as a fundamental part of life skills. Thinking as a skill is described, followed by presenting shades or different modes of thinking. Case studies are then brought in to illustrate how thinking skills can be developed. Facilitators are expected to organize supportive or positive learning environments for the development of these skills. Some activities are also presented for readers to reflect on the main lessons of this chapter.
Chapter 6: Relational and Emotional Skills	Readers are reminded of the impossibility of trying to separate emotions from learning. A case is made for holistic learning, that is, learning that takes into consideration the emotion, the body, the intellect and all that it takes for learners to learn. More discussions are centered on the need to teach learners skills that can help them to modulate their emotions. Case studies are then brought in to illustrate how the emotional and relational skills can be developed. Facilitators are expected to organize supportive or positive learning environments for the development of these skills. Some activities are also presented for readers to reflect on the main lessons of this chapter.

Chapter 7: Essentials of Practical Skills	This chapter explores strategies that can engage learners with the worlds outside their classrooms or schools. This is done for many reasons. The main one being to apply what they learned and hopefully to appreciate the dynamics of real community environment as shaped by reality rather than theories they explore in the classrooms. Case studies are then brought in to illustrate how the practical skills can be developed. Facilitators are expected to organize supportive or positive learning environments for the development of these skills. Some activities are also presented for readers to reflect on the main lessons of this chapter.
Chapter 8: Leveraging Collaborative and Cooperative Skills	Given that we interact with others wherever we find ourselves, cooperation and collaboration are indispensable social skills. In this chapter, therefore, a case is made for developing cooperation and collaboration, the skills that will help us to work in unity—as teams, as partners and as citizens. Case studies are then brought in to illustrate how these skills can be developed. Facilitators are expected to organize supportive or positive learning environments for the development of these skills. Some activities are also presented for readers to reflect on the main lessons of this chapter.

Chapter 9: Honing Social Responsibility Skills	Being responsible is presented as an important community skill. Given its importance, facilitators are encouraged to make intentional move to develop this important skill. Other attributes of being responsible are presented. Then, case studies are brought in to illustrate how skills for being responsible can be developed. Facilitators are expected to organize supportive or positive learning environments for the development of these skills. Some activities are also presented for readers to reflect on the main lessons of this chapter.
Chapter 10: Reflections and Important Lessons	This chapter sums up the important lessons learned in this book. The major philosophies behind the idea of effective or functional learning are summarized as well as characteristics of learning systems with capabilities to imbue learners with functional community skills. Rather, a certain type of learners, 'the engaged learners' are said to be a necessary pre-requisite for making possible the development of functional skills. Even with the presence of these learners, the context of learning is incomplete if learners themselves (their characteristics, learning aspirations and cultures) and contents of learning have not been considered. Strategies for developing certain skills are also summarized. These are recapped and a claim is made that they will differ according to where and why learning is taking place.

Chapter 11: The Implementable

This chapter makes conclusions on important lessons such as the model for 'engaging learners' and summarizes the critical goals of learning as well as present assumptions for making learning systems meaningful or usable in our communities. But the chapter stresses that this book does not provide absolute answers to all questions that educators ask themselves as they prepare and engage in effective teaching-learning activities. It does make suggestions of what facilitators can do to develop community skills. These suggestions are made with a full understanding that some facilitators may be constrained by the prescriptive and standardization of learning where they work but this should not prevent those with the desire to engage in functional learning as presented here. If you as an individual commits, there will be more individuals committing and thus we may succeed transforming our learning or educational activities to address important community skills. It is hoped that the model provided helps guide those who commit to developing these skills.

PART 1

GOALS, CONTENTS AND CONTEXTS

Part 1 introduces readers to the rationale and reasons for writing this book. It explains the background that led to the author wanting to share her experiences of teaching in a field of adult education with a strong preference for community development or community skills. Chapters in this Part outline the philosophies and principles driving the main concept of 'engaged learners'. The concept itself is defined. A model of engaging learners and developing community skills starts to emerge as the two critical concepts of context and content are discussed. This model is elaborated or gets better clarified as the discussion of process and outcome starts to unfold. Also, the literature is brought in to help illustrate, clarify or bring in new and interesting points. Case studies are used to illustrate the main teaching or lessons in each chapter.

CHAPTER 1
AIMS AND TARGETS

If you want education, you must not cut it off from the social interest in which it has its living and perennial sources (Tawney, 1926:22).

Introduction

Not many of us ever get the chance of sharing their teaching-learning experiences with others. This book shares my many years of teaching as an adult educator in higher institutions of learning (colleges of education and university). Although the experiences are said to be specific to these contexts, lessons from these can be applied across different disciplines and educational levels. Actually, strategies for developing the skills that are shared in this book have worked across disciplines and levels of education.

The goals

The main goal for writing this book is to make a case for functional skills. These are skills that learners learn in classrooms and apply to the wider community environment outside the school settings. The development of these skills starts with an understanding that communities and schools interlink or co-exist. That is, learners who go to school are the same people who make up part of the community. They are expected to be meaningfully engaged in these two worlds; schools and communities. Institutions of learning have to fulfill this social duty of linking what is learned with the needs of communities.

Nowadays, community skills are in a danger of being neglected as many universities become more responsive to the labor market (Molesworth, Scullion, & Nixon, 2011). The increasingly use of buzzwords like commercialization of education and the marketization of universities signals a move away from social knowledge, cultural learning or learning in and for the community's way of life. As Molesworth, Scullion and Nixon have observed, today's marketed universities can distort the pedagogical relationship by heralding "a shift from social knowledge to market knowledge" (p. 49). It is the duty of educators to protect the interest of communities and ensure that schooling makes a great impact to these communities. Thus, in this book, the term community skill is used to emphasize need to apply what has been learned in schools to environments outside the four walls of the classrooms.

Communities' values, cultures, lifestyles and needs shape the quality of learning. Likewise, learning gives confidence to communities to sustain themselves. This mutual implication alone prevents learning institutions to close communities out of their missions. They are pressed to think of ways to knit together learning and the larger community's aspirations.

From a rhetoric perspective, many of us understand that learning is a true asset if what happens in institutions is "applied to the social and political conditions present outside its classroom walls" (Searle, 1981:3). Like Searle, many of us wish to see institutions of learning as places "where the textbook is the hoe, the exercise book is the pick; the pencil is the good hammer; and the rest, spade, bucket and screwdriver' (p. 34). All what Searle is saying is that, learning is meaningful if what is learned is acquired in harmony with learners' choice of lifestyle in their respective settings; towns, urban villages, traditional or rural or any other community setting. As already mentioned, many of us have idealized this type of situation for years but as Molesworth, Scullion and Nixon (2011) observe, the "devil tends to have the best tunes as we find comfort being just one of the crowd" (p. 54). Institutions define what and how we teach, even ways of assessment and achievements thus everything is standardized. In some situations, flexibility is restricted as we just have to be like others. However, I believe facilitators can still exercise their originality in their tight situations and become critics of what wheels away our institutions from serving communities.

Important principles guiding the discussions in this book

There are important principles that guide the discussions in this book. Among these are the following:

Learning activities are a reflection of community's ways of life
> Very often, discussions in our classrooms are focused on communities' ways of life like agricultural production, entrepreneurship, unemployment, violence, economic hardships, the culture of socialization, the acquisition and use of literacy, the political structures and functions, history and its importance, the formation and functions of movements and societies, the structure and function of families, community resources and their use, leadership structures and functions, etc. Learning is meaningless or ill-focused if it does nothing to do with these community topics. Thus, our greatest goal as educators is to produce learners with general understanding of these challenges and broad skills to face them.

Reliance on textbooks alone is not an option. Community is seen as a pool of diverse options for learning.

Learners are actively engaged as managers and directors of changes in communities

Engaged learners' goal is to acquire knowledge and skills to face challenges of their lives. Every time when they are taught, they are on the look out of what is meaningful and applicable to real life situations. Their precious time should not be taken away by learning that does not make any reference to how lives are lived in worlds outside the classrooms. They want to acquire skills to help them manage changes that are inevitable in their lives and communities.

Learners' engagement is promoted by applying what they learned to worlds outside their immediate learning environments (the classrooms)

At times engaging learners in class can be challenging. It takes well-trained educators to provide meaningful learning tasks. Advocates for lifelong learning and cultural education, for example, have said educators who explore social issues instantly awaken learners' eagerness and make them enthusiastic to learn. When learners, for example, explore survival means, they emerge with attributes for living or responding to life challenges.

Learning mirrors learners' differences and uniqueness

Learners are different or highly heterogeneous. They exhibit diverse cultural orientations/backgrounds as well as learning experiences and needs. Learning environments have to respect these differences.

CHAPTER 2

THE CONCEPT OF AN 'ENGAGED' LEARNER

> Learners do most of the work. They use their brains, studying ideas, solving problems, and applying what they learn. To learn something well, it helps to hear it, see it, ask questions about it, and discuss it with others (Silverman, 1996).

Introduction

The concept of 'engaged' learner is explained and linked to related concepts of applied learning, active learning, purposeful learning and lifelong learning. Regardless of how we define our learners, what is important for educators is to ensure learners' active engagement. Learning that concentrates on concepts, ideas and theories alone at the expense of application to worlds outside schools falls short of fully engaging them.

Delineating our learners

Many words and phrases are used to describe learners as we think we know them. The word engaged is preferred in this book. It draws attention to the need to see learners becoming immensely engaged in learning as resources, innovators and actors in their own learning processes. The concept of 'engaged learner' is not remarkably different from familiar concepts such as active learners, lifelong learners and adult learners. A brief look at other concepts indicates that they support and complement each other.

Concept	Understanding
Lifelong learners	Lifelong learners learn continuously, thus, learning cannot be thwarted by age or the passage of time. It is a holistic learning, including intellectual, social, physical and emotional development. It is manifested through both formal and informal education (Patsalides, 2011). Lifelong learners are people who take responsibility for their own learning and are prepared to invest "time, money and effort in education or training on a continuous basis (West, 1998).
Adult learners	Adult learners see education as a process of developing increased competence to achieve their full potential in life. They want to be able to apply whatever knowledge and skill they gain today to living more effectively tomorrow. They are people who are performance-centered in their orientation to learning (Knowles, 1973).

Active learners	Active learners energetically strive to take a greater responsibility for their own learning. They take a more dynamic role in deciding how and what they need to know, what they should be able to do, and how they are going to do it. Their roles extend further into educational self-management and self-motivation becomes a greater force behind learning (Glasgow, 1996).

Indeed, the definitions above are not strikingly different. Trying to define learners is a way to portray our preferences in terms of the characteristics, nature and situation of learning. All the definitions in the table above emphasize the need to engage learners in their learning—to let them take responsibility for learning; to engage them holistically; to promote their desire to keep on learning and to apply what they have learned.

The 'Engaged' learners

From an adult educator's perspectives, learners can initiate and be movers of their learning processes although they appreciate facilitators' guidance. The reason for using the word engaged is precisely to underscore this important role and involvement of learners as they learn in classrooms; as well as when applying their learning to settings other than the classrooms. We shall, therefore, apply the term 'engaged' to describe learners who

- Fully interact with their learning environment (colleagues, teachers, learning resources) in search for learning that makes them useful members of their societies.
- Take initiatives and drive their learning processes.

- Broaden their understanding and development of important skills through application, for example, they learn by discussing, acting out, interactive friendship, through voluntarism or connection with others in other walks of life like home, workplace, church etc.
- Want to apply what they hear and say in the learning environments to their social worlds. Learners know that their thinking become real because they act on it and their actions are internalized and become useful because they reflect on them.
- Have a passion for exploring issues related to problems and challenges of real communities.
- Have clear and defined goals of what they want from learning activities. They make great efforts to go beyond getting good grades to acquiring skills for becoming responsible members of their communities.
- They are forever on the lookout of what they can learn wherever and whenever an opportunity presents itself.

Not alone, with others

Learners are not alone in their classrooms. There are teachers. We use variety of names to describe those who teach. It may not be possible to find just one name that suits a teacher. Kincheloe, Slattery and Steinberg (2000) portray them as "mentors, reflective practitioners, diagnostic professionals, facilitators of personal growth, social activists, action researchers and lifelong scholars" (p. 3). In a teacher, we are not looking for a person to transmit what they know to learners. Rather, we are looking for people to "guide and to organize students' activity; not to control or to impose upon the students" (Kaplan, 2009: 334). Kaplan emphasizes that facilitators' task is not to mould character, rather, "to create the conditions in which students can act in such a way that they learn how to control their habits and anticipate the consequences of certain choices (p. 336).

Effective facilitators know that learners come to school knowing to act; they think, initiative and direct their actions. These natural instincts cannot be forgotten when we get in our classrooms. Learners should not be deprived to use these natural capacities. Dewey (1938) reminds us that indoctrination and control show no respect for personality. The message for educators is that they must not deflate learners' natural instincts as these define their being as active human beings. To teach well, facilitators should draw from these energies in the most fruitful and productive way (Kaplan, 2009). As well, they need the right professional disposition like knowing how to relate well with learners and other skills of effective facilitation.

- What are some of the important characteristics of 'engaged learners'?
- What similarities and differences can you see between learners presented in this chapter and learners that you know?
- How best can you (facilitator) describe your learners?

CHAPTER 3
THE CONTEXT AND CONTENTS

To discuss the issue of context is to 'acknowledge the central role of the subject matter, setting and students' diversity. That is, rather than simply describing ideal or best techniques and strategies for facilitating students' learning, pedagogy must inevitably vary according to the subject matter, the social and physical setting where learning is supposed to take place and the individual talents and proclivities of the learners (Davis, 1993).

Introduction

This chapter presents two concepts that cannot be avoided when issues of learning are discussed. These are content and context. Let us start by making some claims, that, 'content is nothing on its own. It only exists as part of context' (Flores & Day, 2006). Flores and Day go on to enlighten us by saying that 'context both defines and enriches content. Without that context, the content is poorer'. We may further appreciate the relationship between content and context within a framework of Hughes and More's (1997) contention that to be effective, learning must be acquired in harmony with our own cultural values, identity and choice of lifestyle, whether we reside in an urban, traditional community or homeland center. These authors remind us that learning does not take place in a vacuum. There is a place (a physical setting), perhaps a home, community and workplace in an urban, semi-urban or rural area. People in these physical settings have their own cultural values, identity and choice of lifestyle that shape the content to be learned. Each of these main concepts is explained below with some illustrations to make it clearer.

Contexts

Learning takes place within specific contexts. Context has been described differently though in a complementary manner by different authors. Brown, Bovey and Chen (1997), for example, define it as the location, time of day, season, temperature, etc. On the other hand, we see Ryan, Parcoe and Morse (1997) defining it as a location, environment, identity and time. Dey (1998) too brings in the idea of emotional state in the definition of context. In a nutshell, context is a place where learning takes place, including the relationship or interaction of those in that particular learning environment.

Learning contexts differ according to where you and your learners are. In these contexts, learners bring diverse backgrounds—their cultures, aspirations, goals and interests. Thus, institutions of learning can be described as contexts "where people of diverse backgrounds coexist" (Mabokela & Madsen, 2009:211). There is, therefore, need for facilitators to be contextually competent. A person with contextual competence is the one who understands the 'broad social, economic and cultural setting' in which learning takes place (Stark, Lowther & Hagerty, 1987). The case below sheds more light on our understanding of context.

Case 1: Understanding the concept of context

To try to illustrate what context is may not be that easy. However, the following illustration may help.

> A literacy assistant says, 'I know that in my teaching, I have to look inside the cultures of my learners; the way they live, their food, language and dressing. Currently, the community I work for is cut out from modern communication and other amenities such as main employment sectors and some important resources. Life is tough for them.

Analyzing Case 1A

- Displaying contextual competence—First, we have been reminded that effective facilitators are those who make efforts to understand the social context of learning. This has been explained as the ability to understand the 'broad social, economic and cultural setting' in which learning takes place. At least we see the facilitator in Case 1 displaying this competence.
- Relating context to content—What is taught in class should be well matched with the realities of the setting in which such learning takes place. When the facilitators are aware of the social, political and cultural contexts, they are able to see how these can become part of the contents of learning. The literacy assistant, for example, has explained that she works in a rural place that is still underdeveloped. We hope this understanding will help her decide on important subject matter that can be of immediate benefit to the learners living in that particular community.

- Considering learners' aspirations or interests—We learned that during one lesson, when the facilitator asked learners what they wanted to learn. Learners indicated a desire to know about modern telecommunication technology, to be precise, cellphones. *'We want to learn about cell-phones'*, said one learner who was thereafter supported by others.
- Contextual deficiency need to be avoided. This deficiency can lead to inappropriate learning content, relationships and ill-defined goals for learning.
- The characteristics of the broader community also matter when issues of context are discussed. In Case 1, readers are made aware of the development status of that particular community. A contextual competent facilitator will examine this environment from 'variety of vantage points, historical, social, economic, psychological, political and philosophical" (Stark, Lowther & Hagery, 1987: 30) and see how it is used to shape the learning activities.
- As Davis (1993) says, context is all about the social and physical setting where learning takes place and the individual talents and proclivities of the learners that shape this particular learning. It is imperative that the facilitators should be contextually competence.

Contents

Content is what learners learn. This, as already explained, include real life situations like employment status, health issues, political situations and crime. Some contents are contained in books while others can be accessed through learners themselves and the communities (e.g. home, community itself, workplaces, national and international environments).

In this book, it is suggested that;

Learning contents are people's ways of life

Content is nothing else but people's actions as they respond to the real life challenges. Examples of some of these challenges are given below.

Children and youth

Issues surrounding youth and children are worth discussing in our classes. In the African countries like Botswana where people are concerned with the problems of violence, crime, substance abuse and infirmity, youth are countered in great numbers. Thus, these aspects should be at the center of learning. Learners have to be aware of them, discuss them as they affect them and the whole nation.

Equality and democracy

The struggle for fairness is an important topic of learning. There is much talk about democracy as fairness in our communities, but very little actions demonstrate this ideal. Searle (1981) has actually observed that "there is danger that the democracy within school is only school democracy inapplicable to the reality outside" (p. 3). Discussion on democracy, for example, would be most profitable to Africa when attention is paid to issues of poverty. Learning, for example, should be focused on questions such as 'how are learning institutions prepared to help learners face the challenge of poverty?' Learning is actually the best tool to imprint in the minds of learners that working together in harmony can help communities develop comprehensive strategies to fight unjust behaviors and actions.

Political confidence

The politics of a nation are great learning content. Perhaps lessons on politics would work best for Africa if learners are educated to understand that without production and the necessary national material base, there is no prospect for economic development. Furthermore, Africa needs political education that will imbue in the mind of learners that politicians are to serve people with trust and loyalty. As Searle (1987) said, they are not educated elite improving their minds on the backs and sweat of their people. They must be out there where people are, teaching and learning with them.

Gender Issues

The situation of equal treatment of males and females should be given some attention in learning. As of now, women's level of participation in the education, politics, economy and leadership positions has suffered since the colonial time in most African countries. This situation has to be discussed alongside a dominant culture of patriarchy that still persists in some African communities. Patriarchy is a cultural thinking that accords prestige to men over women. It gives us insights into a number of gender inequalities, for example, why the most world leaders are men, why some family traditions make it necessary that women take the names of their husbands and children to always carry their fathers' last name (Rose-Innes, 2006). In a nutshell, patriarchy is a philosophy used to oppress, discriminate and exploit females. There is, therefore, need to initiate some discussions around this issue of women's status.

In sum, learners should explore challenges and experiences in the community (individuals, community, national and international). In this way, it is hoped that what is learned can be applied in real life encounters.

A model for content development

The sample content framework presented above gives an idea of sources. Facilitators in their respective environments can do the same for their learners, that is, to come up with contents that they know leaners will relate with. The model presented is just an example.

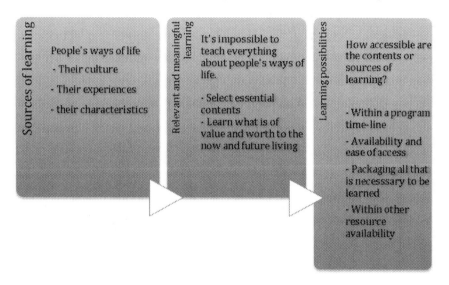

As is illustrated, facilitators have to make decisions about what constitute important learning contents. They should not recommend narrow or limited contents that do not appeal to learners' interest. In truth, decisions of this nature are not easy to make as there are many factors that influence learning progresses. The model should help in the selection of relevant and meaningful contents.

CHAPTER 4
THE PROCESS AND OUTCOME

What we simply call learning is a multitude of processes (Gilman, 1984).

Introduction

This section describes two critical aspects of learning, process and outcome. CHEA (2003, p. 5) defines learning outcomes as the knowledge, skills and abilities that learners attain as a result of engaging in a learning experience. Certainly, we learn hoping to achieve something from the learning experience and this aspect is the outcome.

Process refers to all that goes on to help learners learn, that is, the implementation exercise. Actually, Gilman (1984) likens it to a task of completing a jigsaw puzzle—you need some pieces in place to realize that others are missing. He refers to these missing pieces as concepts, skills and perceptions that help learners grasp the contents. From his metaphor of a jigsaw puzzle, it is clear that the learning process has some general patterns and principles to follow. Gilman further explains that if what is learned is simple to grasp, then, the process of putting the pieces together is easily completed but a complex task requires a lot more pieces to look for. The learning process may, therefore, be viewed as a series of actions or activities that learners engage in, in order to learn or acquire some knowledge and skills. The process is never the same.

The Process

The process refers to the manner in which learning activities are run. It gives answers to a number of questions such as 'How does learning take place?' 'How are the learning goals achieved?' A learner interacts with the contents, with other learners and all present in the learning environment specifically to make meaning out of a particular content. Marks et. al. (2001) would view these types of interactions as learners' interdependent acts that convert inputs to outcomes through cognitive, verbal and behavioral activities directed towards achieving the goals of learning. For most of us, learning process is all about letting learners engage in discussion, acting out situations, solving problems, analyzing problems, thinking and questioning alternatives. It is an active interaction, the synergy of which produces rich learning.

The learning process starts with an understanding of what to learn. The presumption is that once learners have a clear understanding of what they want to learn, then, they can eagerly participate in the learning experiences. They do this by sharing ideas, experiences and some practices. In a nutshell, learning becomes a process of interaction in all its forms, like question-and-answer, group discussion, dramatization, problem solving, experimenting, dialogue, etc. The interactions are physical, intellectual, emotional and spiritual. It is a complex process of discovering, acquiring, changing and developing new knowledge, skills, attitude and behaviors and finding out how these are helpful in one's life. We should always remember that we attend schools to gain capabilities to apply in real life situations like homes, workplaces, churches and other community environments.

Using an analogy to further define the process

To further shed more understanding on the discussion of a process, I conclude with an analogy of a mountain.

Case 3: Analogy of a mountain

Suppose you set on a journey to reach the peak of the mountain. Are you going to see yourself just on top? No. You will need to take routes and precautions to ensure that you get there safely and timely. At times, it may be difficult to reach the peak because the roads or paths are impossible to travel. You may even need to change your plans because they cannot work. Still, it may take you longer time than you expected, making you feel exhausted to continue. In short, the process that you take to reach your learning goals is, in most situations, more demanding.

The analogy of mountain helps us to understand learning as a complex process. There are patterns, steps and actions to go through in order to emerge victorious. Do all of us appreciate this process?

There are times when some learners simply do not appreciate learning as a process. Some, as long as they get high grades, they will not care about the process they have to go through to get those grades. Among these learners are those who would appreciate notes dictated to them by their facilitators rather than going out to explore and meaningfully learning from real environments. In cases where the learning process is taken for granted, facilitators are at times queries for expecting learners to be directors of their learning. Case 4 below gives an example.

Case 4: Process Unappreciated

Doing a social work program, learners were asked to identify a group of street children and for a week work and discuss with them how life was outside their homes and what it was inside their homes. The goal was to make a profile of what made them stay in the street and what made them run from homes. The information was going to be presented in class to strengthen the discussion of a topic, 'The role of families in keeping their children safe at home'. There was one learner who did not see this exercise being consistent with her idea of the fastest way of getting grades. She wanted to take the minimum years to complete her Bachelor of Social Work and would not want to be bothered by assignments that would take 'forever' to be completed. The learner expressed her concern for content coverage because looking at the course outline, it seemed time was running out to cover some topics.

Analysis of Case 4

The case below demonstrates clearly that the facilitator and this particular learner have different orientations to learning. Let us analyze them.

Learner's orientation	Facilitator's orientation
The outcomes of learning like grades matters more than some processes of getting them.	The process of learning is more important than final grades.
Teacher is the container and giver of what is to be learned, learners receive this to emerge victorious.	Prefers learning through actions and learners taking responsibility of their learning.
To be successful in learning, both learner and teacher have to be present in a physical learning environment.	Desires to see learners learning through real life situations, thus valuing activities that take learners to reach learning contexts outside the classrooms.
To have learned is to complete the course outline as planned.	Believes that learning devoid of local issues is inadequately as real learning needs.
The learner demonstrates an 'outcome-oriented' learning	The facilitator illustrates 'a process-oriented learning.

Learners who understand learning as a process get to appreciate the steps they must go through to achieve their learning goals. It is how we appreciate and handle the process of learning in real situations that makes much difference in the way we learn.

Case 5 demonstrates an instance where the process of learning is appreciated.

Case 5: Process Appreciated

> Learners were asked to identify a home or family to do some 'home-reading' of 15-30 minutes in the evening with children. Parents were expected to be present. The reading topics focused on recent challenges facing the communities. Learners chose topics such as HIV and AIDS, bullying in schools and streets, conflict between children and their parents, suicide, passion killings and others.
>
> The facilitator wanted to give learners opportunities to interact with the community by sharing with families important information based on carefully selected reading topics. One learner was to choose one family and one story to share. Learners were to read the story to children, initiate discussions around the topic and get everyone present involved.

Analysis of Case 5

The facilitator reported that all learners enjoyed the activity. It was a rich learning process that expanded their scope of learning beyond mere theories. They learned to act outside the presence of their facilitator; they made own decision as to which articles to read; and they learned how to negotiate their entry into respective homes. For example, it was necessary for learners to discuss with parents the types of stories they wanted to share and the times for visiting the homes. Certainly, for those learners who were already parents, this assignment was fulfilling as for some, it was a daily chore. Most of the learners were happy to learn in relaxed environments outside classroom rules.

The activity itself helped learners to develop important community skills, like;

- Critical thinking—Possibly, learners and those involved in the reading and discussion of the story asked questions and sought answers about the situation presented. They probably asked questions like 'What does this information teach us about people affected?' Is it accurate? How do people get in situations like these? How do people ensure that they avoid a situation like this? These questions help learners to think in a critical manner. Although people ask questions naturally, being critical is a skill that can be developed with intentional practices, like in Case 5.
- Confidence—Confidence in oneself that 'I can do it' is an important feeling that begets a number of skills, for example, self-directedness, creativity and motivation. Learners who went through their assignment successfully realized that they could handle challenges of learning without close supervision of the facilitator.
- Listening skills—Learners learned to listen to and respected people whose thoughts were based on reality than theories. They have learned to understand that no one has little or no knowledge. The listening skills that they have acquired are important both in and outside their classrooms.

There are many skills that are developed through an assignment like this one explained above. Importantly, this type of assignment 'home-reading' provides the impetus for learners to respond to real life situations in a collaborative manner. They have made excellent use of some readings (stories, poems, essays and books) to get families excited about some topics. Learners too have been excited about sitting down with families and discussing with them the contents of reading. This gave them a whole new feeling of excitement. Clearly, the ideas and thoughts of real people, face-to-face with them, differ from those sourced from books and media.

Quite often, at the end of an activity like 'home-reading', learners are expected to write a report to be graded. Facilitators should be careful not to devalue the importance of the learning process that learners went through by emphasizing the outcome of such a process, that is, the report. If facilitators ask learners to produce a report and if that report is the sole source of grading, then report writing amounts to

- Making learners concentrate on what they may not know how to do well, that is, producing a structured report. For example, in a situation like Case 5, a report will definitely not capture precisely what happened during the 'home-visit reading assignment'—the nuances, gestures and other appreciations that came out spontaneously in real life settings are forced into structured episodes of a pen.
- Learners get trapped into selecting and reporting what they think will earn good grades rather than reporting the actual processes of their learning.
- 'I can't report everything in this paper'—This is the common feeling for learners who understand that a report cannot capture all that goes on in real life settings. Usually, learners are forced to refocus and even manipulate what went on to suit the academic requirements. The big picture gets lost and a compromised one emerges for the sake of fulfilling the requirements of the course.
- The report when used as a sole source of grading may breed bad attitude towards a course as learners who have had great experiences may fail the course or get low marks not

because they did not do well in the field but because they are not conversant with standardized and structured assessments exercises like a report.

In Case 5, the facilitator decided to use the report and at the same time positively valued and rewarded the process of learning. Actually,

- The goal was to assess learners' ability to apply their learning to the real life situations.
- To give learners an opportunity to assess themselves. They were given an assessment tool with a scale of 1-10. They rated themselves and gave evidence supporting the ratings. This exercise was situated in real experiences and immediate process of learning.
- The project also included a written journal where learners documented their experiences in full, for example, nuances such as how they were received, the mood of the discussion, the attitude towards the project itself, etc.
- Learners presented their experiences in class, sharing with others, both positive and negative ones.
- The overall report came in as part of other assessment tools.

The assignment as presented shows that the facilitator indeed recognized the nature of learning as a journey traveled by the learners and their communities. For many of us, it is easy to recognize the process and yet so difficult to acknowledge it as worth grading.

Outcomes

Outcomes are results such as gaining new knowledge or refining old ones, acquiring skills, attitudes and behaviors that can be applied in lager environments outside the classroom learning. Evidence of this type of achievement comes as grades, credentials or certificates. A focus on outcome has led to the use of a phrase 'outcome-oriented learning'.

What is an outcome-oriented learning?

Outcome-oriented learning means both learners and facilitators are more concerned with the end result of learning like grades and certificates and perhaps take little interest in the process of learning.

Ask learners in any learning institution (college, university, vocational schools, etc.) about why they have decided to go schooling, you will probably get similar responses;

- I would like to get my degree in three years and be a successful worker, parent and enjoy my life.

  > Learning is 'becoming'. It is not for now but for the future. The future has a very clear route. You learn, get grades and they get you there! Learners spend time learning to reach well-defined future.

- Well, I am here doing "Space Exploration' (going to the moon) because I don't want to do common jobs. I want my parents to be proud of you.

  > Deeply held belief about learning limited to a tiny imaginary world. The goal for which they have come to learn is to get hold of this 'diamond'. Others are expecting them to succeed, so that should be.

- See, I am here to attend all classes and do all my assignments, hand them on time. So I don't expect to get low marks. I want high marks. I want everyone to be impressed by my transcripts (final grades) so that I don't negotiate the type of job I want. Can't wait to complete my courses!

  > Deeply held belief about high grades as a gateway to living the type of life one so wishes to live and do so well, and, about learning as an activity that can be hurried and well timed.

We can go on and on giving examples of what most learners want from educational or learning experiences. An emerging pattern among the statements given is that of 'learn and proceed to a good future'. Many learners seem to think that there is a straight link between what you do in school and how your future will be. To a certain extent, this makes sense. However, those who are completely (100%) convinced that 'good grades are synonymous with successful life upon completion of school' can be misled. It is an orientation that potentially can make them pay attention to certain subjects that they believe can get them good grades driving them to their ideal future. It becomes easy for them to ignore or not be serious with any subject matter that does not fit their imaginary worlds. This would limit their choices of programs or subjects.

Learners should be made to understand that learning is not only about thinking for an idealized future. The fear is that if they focus solely on how they will live their future lives, they may limit their potential to explore other possibilities. Real life challenges get you into real worlds not imaginary ones. For example, life circumstances can dictate the type of work (job) to engage in. Remember, many people spend the rest of their lives with certificates in hands still looking for that imaginary future. Learners should realize that no one can skip the present to live in the future; they should actively explore present circumstances to see how they shape their imaginary worlds. Like the analogy of a mountain, there may need to change their perspectives by observing trends with present employment and other developments. Also, the analogy of the mountain illustrates that setting goals and meeting the requirements of learning is all about planning, re-planning, changing strategies and moving with time to attend or direct steps towards achieving that which you have planned. Learning too is not a simple process—it is just like the analogy of the mountain presents it.

Input

One important aspect of learning is the input. If we ask ourselves a question 'What do we need to start a learning experiences (a lesson, a course or a program)? This question leads to what is referred here as the input. It has already been mentioned in the beginning of this chapter that there shall be no detailed discussion of the inputs. However, the table below gives guidance as to how to determine what these are. It has been presented as an activity that you can do to indicate what you believe is important.

The following offer important clues as to what can be considered input factors.

Agree	Disagree	Unsure	Who?
			✓ Learning takes place because there are people present to make it happen—the learner, facilitator, other resource like people. ✓ One question to ask when planning or preparation a learning experience is the '**Who**' question, 'Who are the targeted learners? ✓ Make detailed profiles or characteristics of people to be engaged in the learning activity.

			What? A number of questions can be asked, for example, ✓ What makes the learning activity necessary? ✓ What will be learned? ✓ What determine what should be learned? ✓ What sources will you use for learning? ✓ What roles will each person present in the learning activity play? ✓ What possible facilitating and inhibiting factors should facilitators be aware of? ✓ What will learners emerge with from the learning environment? ✓ What evidence of learning will learners have/show?
			Why? A number of questions can be asked, for example, ✓ Why is it necessary to carry out this particular program or learning experience? ✓ Why do you believe people you selected/invited/asked to participate are the right ones for this particular learning activity?

			How? A number of questions can be asked, for example, ✓ How will available resources be used? ✓ How will learning activities and assessment exercises be structured? ✓ How will the learner and facilitator interact? ✓ How will learning be conducted, assessed, monitored and rewarded? ✓ How long will the learning activities take place?
			When? A number of questions can be asked, for example, ✓ When is the learning activity taking place? ✓ When will it start and when will it end? ✓ When will you send out invitation letters or notices for the program/learning activity?

			Where?
			A number of questions can be asked, for example,
			✓ Where is the learning activity taking place?
			✓ Where will people who attend this learning activity come from?
			✓ Where do we get resources and sources for learning from?

This table gives some hints about the types of questions that facilitators may ask when preparing for their learning activities. As the questions show, they answer one great question of how one prepares for a successful learning experience. The questions are not asked in any orderly manner but they are all important. I have also presented the table as a learning activity so that readers can decide which input factors are important in their situations.

Facilitators in some institutions usually do not face dilemma of not knowing how to go about establishing most of these input factors. They are standardized through entry requirements, procedures and pre-existing places for learning (classrooms, lecture rooms, reading rooms, etc.) and calendrial time determined by fees per credit. Institutions go further to even standardize accomplishments through the use of tests; define what are core skills, and pre-specify uniform learning outcomes (Tett, 2006). Tett further observes that this type of standardization makes it necessary that people are ranked from bottom to top with the emphasis on what they cannot rather than what they can do. This leads to a deficit model where those on the bottom rugs are positioned as lacking the skills. In most cases, these standardizations do not accommodate people's own definitions and goals of learning.

- How is the concept of 'out-come' focused learning used?
- What does the concept of 'process-focused' learning mean?
- How possible do you think you can focus on both the outcome and process?
- What activities can you do to make your learners value the process of learning?

PART 2

ENGAGING FOR SKILLS DEVELOPMENT

This section covers chapters 3-7. Each chapter starts with a quote that succinctly captures the gist or intended lesson of the chapter. The chapters themselves present skills that are considered critical for community development. The chapters use case studies to illustrate and describe the skills being promoted.

It is important that educators engage learners holistically. Holistic learning means engaging "the body, emotions, attitudes and physical well-being" of the learners (Jensen, 2008:82). The engagement basically transforms learners. They emerge with skills and a sense of ownership of learning and responsibility to use what has been learned to make a difference in their lives, those of their families, community, work and other environments. The goal is to engage learners meaningfully in developing skills like thinking, cooperation, collaboration, relational, emotional, being responsible and practical. Indeed, like Hargreaves (2003) advises, learning should cultivate these capacities as well as "develop deep cognitive learning, creativity and ingenuity among students, drawing on research, working in teams . . .

promoting problem-solving, risk taking, trust in the collaborative process and ability to cope with change and commitment to continuous improvement" (p. 3). Chapters in this section are a guide to how to develop these community skills.

The teaching-learning strategies that can be used to develop these functional skills are also identified, defined and described. The rationale for using a particular strategy is explained in relation to how it integrates and promotes specific community skills. Tips are provided for how best to use the strategy. Facilitators are, however, expected to come up with other relevant strategies.

Strategies provided in this book are to be applied in a flexible manner. They can be modified to suit the knowledge or skills that one wants to develop. Educators should make their choices of teaching-learning strategies carefully. The choice of strategies should also be guided by the principle of variability. This means that we should expose learners to different learning activities; exercise their thinking capacities; provide opportunity for them to apply what they have learned; give them exercises that appeal to their emotions and attitudes; and make them physically involved in learning.

CHAPTER 5
THE BRAIN—'PEDAGOGICS OF THINKING'

When reason fails you, imagination saves you! When intuition fails you, your reasoning saves you. There are many ways of engaging in thinking (Davis, 1993).

Introduction

The word brain is used here analogically to refer to the use and development of the thinking capacities. Indeed, learners think all the time. It is precisely because they are expected to think that a chapter has been devoted to strategies of helping them to do so in a fruitful and effective manner. Like Nickerson says, all facilitators want "students to become good thinkers because thinking is at the heart of what it means to be human" (Nickerson cited Davis, 1993:174). Thus, promoting learners' thinking capacities is "one of the most important goals of our teaching" (Davis, 1993:173).

Thinking is a fundamental part of life skills. A primary focus on it directs our attention to creativity, reasoning, being adaptive and reflective. These are attributes needed everywhere (e.g. in schools, at homes, in workplaces; Yes, everywhere). Facilitators are expected to organize supportive or positive learning environments for the development of thinking skills.

Thinking as a pedagogical issue

Thinking as a skill is defined in different ways. For example, scientific thinking as Dewey would call it is "the mental habit of free inquiring, tolerance of alternative viewpoints and free communication" (Dewey cited in Jenlink, 2009: ix). As presented in the graphic illustration that follows, thinking takes different shades. Some are discussed in this chapter while others are left to facilitators to think about in their respective settings.

Thinking skills at a glance

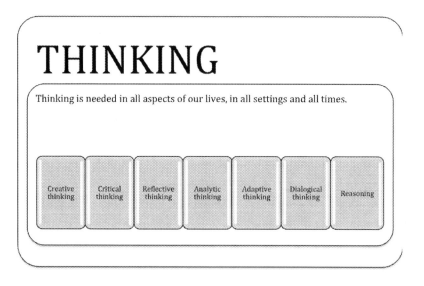

Developing thinking skills

Facilitators who intend to develop thinking skills should plan for this. Below is an example of how one facilitator introduced the importance of thinking skills.

Case 6: The importance of the thinking skills

At the beginning of the first class, the facilitator implored learners to always think when being taught, when learning and when doing their assignments. He said, 'by coming to class everyday, making your presence, you will not learn. Learners do not learn by listening to facilitators only but by engaging their thinking skills. Think! Think! Think!" He continued to say' "When you think, you learn how to question, when you ask questions, it shows you are reasoning and when you reason, you will make meaningful arguments. When you make meaningful arguments, you gain new knowledge, when you gain new knowledge, you tend to challenge what others think or say and you will be able to question claims made by others and yourself. Engaging your thinking skills will help you question more how the information you gain in class can help you in your life.

You need to think about how you may use what you have learned, that is, think about the worth of what you are learning. In this way, you will make intelligence contribution both in and outside the classroom'. When discussing a variety of topics, for example, some controversial ones like crime and poverty. You need to engage deepest level of thinking. Thinking will help you to always develop some new perspectives, that is, look at issues from different perspectives; yes, this is possible if you think. Let us all make thinking our habit. Think! Think! And Think!'

Analyzing Case 6

After reading the scenario presented, you will agree with me that thinking is what we do most in our learning activities. Yes, we know that naturally everyone thinks but we also know that there is a level of thinking that we want our learners to reach and it is our obligation to promote it.

Going over the scenario, you will realize that indeed there are levels or types of thinking that the facilitators should aspire to see their learners demonstrating. A quick look at these may help us understand why this particular facilitator emphasizes the need for learners to think, he said, 'Think! Think! Think!

Thinking skills that emerge from Case 6

The statements have been taken as they are in Case 6 and used to indicate the shades of thinking coming out from what the facilitator said.

Skills	Description as is in the case
Reasoning skills	If you ask questions, it shows you are reasoning and if you reason, you can make meaningful arguments. This is an aspect of thinking.

Creative thinking	Developing new perspectives, looking at issues from different angles and making important new conclusions is a way of thinking. Coming up with new perspectives is an indicator of thinking creatively.
Critical thinking	When you argue, you are challenging what others think or say, you question claims made by others and yourself too. Questioning claims illustrates that a person is thinking critically and responding appropriately.
Dialogical thinking	You will make meaningful argument by defending ideas logically—this indicates that thinking is going on.
Adaptive thinking	When you think of application, you are thinking more about how you may use your knowledge, that is, you are thinking about the worth of what you are learning. In this way, you are likely to make intelligent contribution both in and outside the classroom.

You will agree with me that skills presented in the table above are very important. They help to make learning interesting as everyone gets engaged. Thinking itself is fundamental because "to function in any society, one must learn to think; thinking is a key survival skill" (Davis, 1993:175).

I guess, if you may ask learners to come up with instances where they thought they have really engaged their thinking skills or someone has exercised his or her thinking skills, there will be many examples. If you have not thought about the importance of thinking, ask yourself this question, 'Can you act before thinking?' 'How long can you take without thinking? I will leave these questions for you to think about.

How then can we develop thinking skills?

There are numerous ways of developing thinking skills. Here I share just some few strategies that have worked well for me and facilitators who used them.

In-basket approach

With a very clear understanding of the topic of discussion and the learning activity, the facilitator writes the main arguments/ideas on strip of papers. These will be folded and placed in a container, herein called 'a basket'. For example, supposing the topic of the discussion is 'What is poverty?' The facilitator interested in getting learners' views through guided discussion will prepare phrases or statements to lead the discussion such as those listed below;

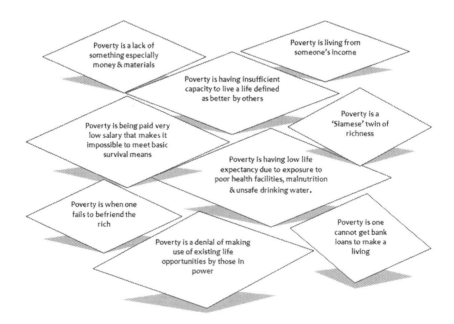

As the list of options above indicates, this strategy is about placing as many ideas/thoughts/problems as possible in a 'basket' (a container) from which learners choose the ones that appeal to their interest and thinking. The important thing is that the facilitator has to be very clear of the topic of discussion and the objectives for teaching such as topic. The in-basket is usually more interesting in controversial or topics requiring argument or those that attract variety of perspectives like topics around the issue of poverty. Facilitators may use it in the beginning, middle or when they wrap up their learning activities.

Below is presented a detailed case of how this strategy may be used.

Case 7: Using the In-basket Strategy

In a class that I taught as an adult educator, 'Adult Education and National Development', I found myself using the in-basket more often than other strategies simply because I felt that most of the issues discussed were controversial or problematic, for example, democracy as lived in the country, levels and conditions of poverty, crime and other issues that affect the development of a country. These topics challenged the minds of learners.

One day I posed a challenge to learners;

'I want you to think about what is currently going on in our country. We read newspapers days in and out, every single month and year. We hear about deaths of lovers when we walk the streets, when we ride public transport and in our classes. Young people are killing each other in what seemed to be a 'fashionable' crime called passion killing. Let us discuss how this act affects our nation. Let us hear how it affects us as families, friends, communities, individuals, etc.'

This activity was given to kick start learners' thinking ability. Learners were expected to question the logic of 'passion-killing' and think about what could possibly lead to this unbecoming action. They would have to argue; debate and visualize how this action impacted the lives of people affected as well as the nation that had to deal with it. After learners internalized the problem, then an in-basket exercise was introduced. This involved developing a number of alternative ideas or solutions to be considered.

In this case, the in-basket was used to get learners think about possible alternatives to ending or minimizing the crime of passion killing. Thus, the 'basket' contained different alternatives that guided the learner to debate around the possible solutions. The Facilitator prepared them to guide learners' discussion. The following were example of options in the 'basket'.

- More parental involvement in the love affairs of their children—so that when the problems arise, children can freely and quickly share them with parents.
- An eye-for-an-eye—That all those who kill should be severely punished.
- Awareness training for lovers—The workshop can be held for young people to be made aware of a number of issues, for example, what it takes to get themselves involved in love relationships, how to spot problems before they worsen and how to avoid to be counted in the statistics of having 'done it' or being a victim.
- Counseling and rehabilitation for the affected may be necessary.

These are just some examples of what was in the 'basket'. Learners were then divided into small groups (5-10) and asked to choose what they believed was the best or the worse option for addressing the problem. The groups were then asked

- To come up with reasons for their choice
- Cite examples, if applicable, where their option has worked
- To indicate aspects that can impede or facilitate the actions suggested by the option selected
- Present and defend their position in class.

Analyzing Case 7

As intended, this type of activity is good for promoting learners' thinking capacities, for example,

- Learners have to give reasons for choosing one option over the others. This also calls for them to prepare for and defend their position. This is a way of developing reasoning skills.
- Learners will go through this exercise effectively if they reflect on what has happened not only in their country but elsewhere where the problem has been experienced. They reflect on the present and past experiences and how the victims, communities, state, groups or organizations with interest would handle this problem. This helps develop their reflective thinking.
- Learners are expected to weigh the advantages against the disadvantages of an option given. They discuss and argue among themselves to come to a conclusion about the one option they prefer. They analyze issues critically and this helps them develop critical thinking skills.

- The main goal of an exercise like this one is to see if learners can come with intelligent reasons pertaining to how a problem may be addressed. They come to see the logic or illogic of their thinking as other learners comment on their responses. This is a way of promoting their problem-solving skills and tolerance of constructive critics.
- Learners are bound to exercise their creative skills as they think of ways to make their option unique and different from those of other groups. They bring new ideas to justify their choices thus in one way or the other, the exercise calls for and helps develop their creative thinking.
- Also, the exercise calls for everyone's contribution. Learners talk among themselves. They listen to each other. They say what they are thinking. It's all about engaging everyone in a dialogue. It is a way of exercising dialogical and logical skills.

If learners are committed to doing an exercise like the one above, their thoughts are seriously provoked. It becomes so easy for the facilitator to see that indeed learners are fruitfully engaged. They make productive noises and arguments about the problem and its possible solutions. This type of engagement supports the philosophy of 'engaged' learners presented in this book. It speaks of the need for facilitators to let learners exercise their free thinking, independent from facilitators' influence and direction. Importantly, this type of learning activity has an in-built way of teaching learners that, in life there are different alternatives/options to solving a problem. This becomes very clear to them as they compare options given by different groups.

Other important points coming from case 7 include

- Learning content does not sever its connection from real life situation. Learners are made to discuss a problem happening in their country. Thus, the learning activity becomes interesting, meaningful and provides a high teachable or learning moment for the learners and facilitators.

- Learners are engaged with what they can relate to or identify with. It becomes interesting for them to explore options for addressing a problem like this one. It gives them a sense of being responsible.

Throughout this book, there is an attempt to illustrate the importance of contents that learners can relate with.

Tips for discussing sensitive topics

Every time when we teach, we "must be aware of not only what we say but also how we say what we say'. It is important to understand that what we say has much positive impact as how we say" (Friedman, 2005:2). This phrase is a reminder that we can build or sustain our relationship of working together with our learners if we are sensitive to what we say and how we communicate it.

There are times, when facilitators have to discuss sensitive issues. It is important that they connect learners to the topic in a manner that brings the best learning out of the topic. For example, when we discuss a sensitive topic like the one discussed in Case 7: Passion Killing, we should first of all make learners appreciate the importance of discussion this type of topic. If the topic is not carefully introduced to the learners, the discussions may evoke negative emotions or attitude. For example, those who have been affected may feel offended or mocked.

Certainly, sensitive topics cannot be avoided in our learning environments especially in adult education. Rather, they have to be tackled with care. Most facilitators should be equipped to deal with these types of topics. Facilitators are known for changing their 'hats' to address specific learning challenges. They act as parents, counselors, spiritual healers and friends. They change functions to suit special situations.

Facilitators would not want to be caught unaware, having forgotten the right 'hat' to wear to suit the discussion of that particular sensitive topic. Imagine introducing a sensitive topic like passion killing and regretting ever introducing it as emotions get out of hand—what do you do? Do you stop the discussion or what? No facilitator would like to be caught in a situation like this. I once joked with my colleague about how to respond to some of these highly charged emotions in our classes. My colleague responded, 'if students cry, I will run away and perhaps will not want go back to that class again'. Well, fleeing may not be a good choice for the facilitator, but perhaps other options are there. Importantly, we need to be prepared to 'wear the right hat for a special moment'.

Tips for using the in-basket

If you intend to use an 'in-basket' as a pedagogical strategy to 'put the brain at work' (promote critical thinking, reflection, creativity, skills of describing, defining, analyzing and explaining), always

- Give learners enough background knowledge to enable them to use the strategy well, for example, describe the strategy to the learners and explain why you believe such strategy is suitable for the exercise at hand.
- Explain how the strategy helps in achieving the objectives of that particular lesson.
- Make clear to the learners what will make the strategy work for them (what you expect learners to do).

- Ensure that the activity is clearly explained and everything to make it successful has been made available to the learners.
- During presentation, encourage learners to cross-check or compare their option with those of other groups, e.g. what could have led to the different perspectives/options.
- Always provide feedback on learners' presentation and summarize the critical points of the lesson in a manner that accentuate how the objectives of the lesson have been achieved.
- Get feedback from learners about how they feel about the use of the strategy in class (in-basket) and its benefits outside class.

As with all instances of learning where learners' interest and motivation are evoked, when using the in-basket approach, learners usually feel challenged and time is never sufficient for them to complete the activity. Each one of them wants to be heard and to be convinced about how his or her contribution feeds into the overall alternative or strategy for solving the problem. You may, therefore, want learners to continue exercising their thinking outside the class time.

Another strategy that can be used for promoting the thinking capacity is the 'word-play'. This strategy is explained below.

Word-play games

As the names implies, this strategy helps learners to use words, find their associations and meanings as well as describe critical characteristics that make one to understand the main concept being discussed. In short, the strategy is usually used to teach new concepts. A concept is a string of ideas (conceptskills.wikispace.com).

It is assumed that each field of study has particular concepts that need to be taught and learned. These concepts may be theories, philosophies and other ideologies. Usually, learners do not know these upon entry into a discipline or field of study. Thus, this strategy works well when helping learners to understand some of these critical concepts.

The art of teaching concept is sometimes referred to as building conceptual skills. Stark, Lowther and Hagerty (1987) define conceptual skills as "understanding the theoretical foundation of the profession" (p.19). They emphasize that learners need to learn the generally accepted foundational knowledge upon which a professional practice is based.

Word games for developing thinking skills

Word-games are many. In here, I use a puzzle, one of the familiar word games in the teaching-learning environments.

In this particular case, a puzzle can be given following a short conversational lecture with some learners. The conversational lecture provides learners with information as in Case 8.

Case 8: Short Conversational lecture

> One valuable concept or theory available for deepening our understanding about adult learners is that of andragogy. Malcolm Knowles came up with this theory after years of teaching adults learners. I guess every learner in the field of adult education has to know this theory as compared with pedagogy. In

this theory, Malcolm Knowles describes adult learners as learners who

- bring to the learning situation attitudes and characteristics that are different from those of children and adolescents
- are self-directed and the facilitator is there to guide rather than control learning
- bring some experiences to the learning situation. They value and use these experiences as learning contents more than information packaged in books and other sources.
- respect real life situations and problems as creating a readiness for them to learn and shape other practical encounters
- want to apply immediately what they learn, that is, they are performance-centered in their orientation to learning.

These points are just examples of a detailed lesson that the facilitator can give on this concept of andragogy. The lesson, for example, also can include the confidence that adult learners have learning about real life problems. Learning activities that appeal to personal experiences and curiosity to learn something new are some of the characteristics of adult learners. It is important to understand that although they are mature to work on their own, guidance from the facilitator is needed. A safe and conducive environment for them is when they realize that their learning goals are addressed.

After a short conversational lecture with learners covering all pertinent details as illustrated above, about this concept of andragogy, learners can now be given a puzzle to work on. They now have information to use to solve a puzzle.

Case 9: The puzzle

This is a simple word-play to serve as an example here. Facilitators can develop more demanding ones with multidirectional search.

S	A	F	E	A	P	P	L	I	C	A	T	I	O	N
T	E	D	I	N	D	E	P	E	N	D	E	N	C	E
S	E	L	F	D	I	R	E	C	T	E	D	E	G	O
C	O	N	T	R	O	L	L	I	N	G	A	M	E	S
I	R	O	M	A	T	U	R	E	A	L	I	T	Y	O
E	N	G	A	G	E	D	I	C	T	A	T	E	L	L
N	O	T	E	O	R	G	A	N	I	S	E	R	V	E
T	H	I	N	G	O	A	L	O	N	T	X	N	E	W
I	D	E	A	Y	O	U	N	G	R	A	P	P	L	E
F	A	C	T	U	A	L	E	A	R	N	E	R	S	E
I	N	T	E	L	L	I	G	E	N	C	E	A	G	N
C	U	R	I	O	S	I	T	Y	E	S	T	A	R	T
P	P	I	L	E	X	P	E	R	I	E	N	C	E	R
L	P	A	T	I	M	P	O	R	T	A	N	T	A	U
R	E	L	A	T	I	O	N	S	H	I	P	O	T	S
N	R	C	O	N	F	I	D	E	N	C	E	R	A	T

Specific tasks of the activities included,

- Learners are expected to illustrate their full understanding of the concept of andragogy
- They need to think about and find different characteristics or words associated with the concept of andragogy. This demonstrates their understanding of the main concept.
- The selection of words associated with the concept of andragogy also requires them to think about how these words can be used to explain the main concept of andragogy
- Learners are expected to come up with their own descriptions of the main concept of andragogy.

As indicated by the items given above, learning concepts using word game is more than just knowing the meaning of isolated words. It goes beyond this to expect learners to have an accurate and clear image of the main concept being learned. It is about 'knowing the meaning of words and having adequate conscious view of its meaning" (Higginbothan, 1998). For example, in Case 9, those who understood the concept of andragogy well during the conversational lecture would come up with more words from the puzzle to describe it. Words like application, experience, mature, confidence, engage, independence, goal and many others if found in the puzzle should illustrate learners' understanding of the theory or concept of andragogy.

Those of us who have used a word puzzle know that this game is a good exercise for engaging learners' brain (thinking and remembering). The activity keeps each learner actively engaged as she or he searches for relevant words. The important thing for the learner is to see how each word chosen is going to be used. It relaxes learners' focus on the facilitator. They become immersed in the learning activity. They have fun playing or searching for words. They think about how the chosen words useful in the exercise they have been given.

Tips for using the puzzle

- Ensure that learners have the background knowledge to engage in the exercise. This may come from lecturing to them or carefully selecting reading materials for them to provide the necessary background.
- When designing the puzzle, ensure that all necessary words are included. You may want to play it before giving it out to class as a learning activity.
- Direct learners on how to use the puzzle to fork out important word and ensure that there is only one main concept to focus

on. Remember, you may use a single puzzle to explore many subsidiary words.

- As with all other pedagogical strategies, ensure that the strategy is described enough for learners to use it without difficulties.
- Explain the reasons for using this particular strategy.
- Explain clearly the role that learners play in the activity and what will make this strategy work or fail for them.
- Explain how the strategy helps in achieving the objectives of lesson.
- Always provide feedback on learners' work and summarize the critical points of the lesson in a manner that accentuate how the objectives of the lessons have been achieved.
- Get feedback from learners about how they feel about the use of this strategy in class (puzzle) and the skills that they have developed through the use of this exercise. You may go further by asking them why they believe it is important

I am convinced that a puzzle is a useful strategy for teaching learners to think.

Skills developed through Case 9

As part of the specific pedagogy of learning promoted in this book 'An Engaged Learner', you will notice that the puzzle engages learners through thinking in a fun and effective manner. It

- Promotes their comprehension or understanding skills. As they become curious to find relevant words, their concentration skills increase.

- It develops their observation skills—the word play has a pattern and learners can do well if they are able to observe and follow this particular pattern.
- It prompts them to use their writing skills—in the Case given, learners were asked to identify words to use in describing or defining the main concept being studied (Andragogy). This in a way helps them to exercise their writing skills as well as to make meaning out of what they have written.
- Comparing and matching skills are also promoted as learners look for and select the right words to fit with others.

These are not the only skills that wordplay can develop. It does, to a great extent develops learners' independence and judgment skills.

The 'What-If' approach

'What-Iffing' is an approach that facilitators can use to promote learners' thinking skills. Harris (2002) explains that this strategy "involves describing an imagined action or solution and then examining the probable associated facts, consequences, or events. Facilitators engage learners' reasonable minds by making them generate implications/consequences of newly imagined incident (virtualsalt.com/crebook2.htm).

Below is one example of how this approach can work.

Case 10: 'What-If' strategy

Facilitator poses a 'What-If scenario, for example,

What if the government stops supporting the poor and ask individuals with interest to do it?

Learners are given the chance to think about this scenario and react to it. They think in a manner that challenges their

- Reasoning skills—Learners are expected to generate new strategies with clear implications or consequences of this imagined new situation.
- Critical thinking—It gives learners opportunity to weigh the possibilities of what can work against what may not work. This means criticizing both what has been the common strategies in relation to newly proposed strategies. Their argument is expected to address the consequences of the new strategy in relation to the role of the government in national development and who 'these individuals' are and what/why they have to be given this responsibility.
- Decision-making skills—learners are expected to analyze the 'what-if' scenario, and develop different strategies based on their understanding of the current. Learners are then expected to respond to the scenario and defend their responses.
- Reflective thinking—learners have to think about what is currently happening, like welfare schemes and other government support for the poor. It is from this understanding that they can start to imagine how it will be if the government directs poverty issues to individuals.

Observation from Case 10

Learners can do very well to address the 'what-if' scenario if they do not have a general understanding of the current situation. In most cases, the strategy will not work well if it is based on abstract concepts or foreign ideas that learners do not understand. Where learners have sufficient information to do the exercise, it can help promote a number of skills including

- Reasoning, arguing, reflection and making decisions, which are important aspect of thinking. If learners fail to think in ways that is considered logical by others, then their reasoning or understanding of the scenario is questioned. This becomes evidence from the questions and comments that other learners make in responding to presenters' arguments.
- Comprehension—learners are expected to understand the scenario. They fail to make logic arguments and reach reasonable decisions if the scenario is not understood or if they have little background knowledge to the exercise.

There are times when you may feel that the 'What-If' scenario has not been well done by learners because of a number of reasons. If lack of background knowledge is the case, I advise that another one be thought of that can help give learners that feeling of success. Learners should not fail to use the strategy. This may create some negative attitude towards using it. Facilitators should not let this happen.

Facilitators can develop a simpler one. For example, in following the "What if the government stops supporting the poor and asking individuals to do it?'; you may present a guided one. An example is given below.

Case 11: Another example of the 'What-If'

What if students are actively involved in strategies for addressing the poor people?

Facilitators are expected to give enough background knowledge for learners to go through this activity successfully. A detailed scenario like the one below may be given.

A group of learners from Village X have been given funds to decide what they can do for their community to address an identified community's need. They were given time to think about it but failed to decide on a specific project within the time limits. Other people in the project decided to think for them.

The funder decided that they should build a recreational hall for the HIV/AIDS patients. The person providing the plot wanted them to start an economic gardening for the villagers so that everyone could buy vegetables cheap and as she argued, this could also provide employment for the villagers who were idling. The business advisor has a different idea. Based on the small number of people in that community, he opted for training community members on some 'how-to' courses that members themselves should choose, for example, how to bake bread, how to grow vegetables, how to keep bees, etc.

Analysis of Case 11

First, the funder said he would drop his intention to fund if learners decided to do something different. Equally, the person who promised the plot was not sure whether she would like something else to be done in her plot. The business advisor also expressed his interest in the 'how-to' training programs as he was best qualified to do them. The learners are to make their choice now. Which one and for what reasons will they go with?

The idea for giving out this activity is to see how learners can think and respond to a challenging situation that demands that they act quickly and intelligently to it. The situation is made complex because each person involved has 'the power' to withhold some important aspects that should help the project to take off. One has financial power. Another has allocation of plot power and the other one, expertise power. Who are learners going to take sides with? Will learners need to compromise or negotiate for what they believe is a better option in order to use the finances? Remember, learners have not been given the option of dropping the project. It is important to the community and has to be implemented.

This scenario above is different from the main one which asks learners to think about, 'What if the government stops supporting the poor and asking individuals to do it?' In the current one, people have made decisions that learners have to agree or disagree with some consequences. It wants learners to think and make the right decision within some tight timelines.

Potential skills promoted by Case 11

The activity given does not entertain self-doubt. Learners need to act and act instantly and with confidence that they will make a sensible choice. This experience among others things calls learners

- To analyze the options they have and make sense of each of them—this is the development of an analytic thinking
- To make important choices—learners have been given a number of choices, so they have to make decisions about which one they prefer, declare their interest and see how others think about them—This, in a way, promotes decision-making and declarative thinking skills
- To negotiate with others who do not share the same thinking or decisions with them. There are three choices from three

different people. Learners are to choose one option and persuade others to buy into it—this is a way of developing their persuasive thinking.

As facilitators, we should be persuaded to give learners more activities that exercise their thinking skills. Thinking skills are diverse and all of them important. We are made to understand that making decision is a way of thinking as well as ability to persuade others to think too.

A metaphor

Sometimes when I do not want to use word games for teaching concepts like theories, I use metaphors or analogies. Some facilitators who have used analogies link them to metaphors, so is the case in this chapter. Commenting on this link, Longknife and Sullivan (2002) indicate that an analogy is really only an extended metaphor. As already mentioned, metaphors are good in developing the thinking skills.

To underscore the importance of using metaphors, Bowers (1993) claims that our thinking is metaphorical and as such metaphors are effective learning tools that are congruent with our natural ways of thinking as human beings.

To use a metaphor, a facilitator may bring to class carefully selected objects. These may come as pictures or real small toy-like objects, as illustrated below. These are selected for "their suggestive qualities, to see what ideas they can break loose, and especially for helping to examine the problem better" (Harris, 2002: virtualsalt.com/crebook2.htm). Thus, these items have to be chosen carefully and variety of them would help give learners options to choose from.

Case 12: Using metaphors to promote learners' thinking skills: An example

Each learner is asked to pick one of these items that resembles what he or she believes comes close to explaining his or her understanding of 'learning'. The activity prompts learners to think about the 'likeness' of a particular object to some life encounter/problems or challenges. As Harris (2002) says, by searching for several points of similarity between the analogy and the problem, new aspects of the problem are revealed and new perspectives come out (virtualsalt.com/crebook2.htm).

After learners select items, the facilitator asks them to describe their analogues.

In one class that I used these metaphors, the level of thinking in learners was amazing. One learner, for example, said,'

 I have picked up a car. A car to me symbolizes what I want to emerge with from my studies. That is, something tangible that I can show the world. I have achieved something. But I know that to have it, I must work hard for it. I must save some money. As a learner, the car for me is like a certificate that I want to emerge with. To have the certificate, I must study very hard to get enough marks or grades. I must ensure that every semester, I save adequate grades to move me to the next one. If my savings are not enough, I know I may not get the certificate. I know that when I let other things disturb me like laziness, truancy and nice time, I may not save enough credits to get what I want. So, I have to be careful. I will work hard to save enough to get me what I want.

The level of thinking is impressing. She demonstrates some creativity and can analyze an object to suit her understanding of why she is in school. She can interpret and give sound reasons for what she has chosen. Other learners were amazing too when it got to their choices as indicated by another example that follows.

'I just happened to have picked this one', he smiled as he showed us a toy of what looks like a small boy but with features of an old man like beard and grey hair. I don't know, this learner said, but I think at times I find myself confused, like, this boy is showing some confusion. I ask myself questions about the usefulness of schooling when I see some people who are rich but have not been to school. For me, I believe learning is all about taking out the confusions that we have. For example, this boy needs to be cleaned up and be himself. I feel I don't want anyone to confuse me about the importance of school. I have to ask questions but that phase has to pass and should know what I am looking for. Because when you are confused, no one understands you and you will not understand yourself either. This feeling takes you nowhere and you can't move anywhere.

Analyzing Case 12

There are a number of important lessons coming out from the case above. First and foremost, you will realize that when using metaphors as a teaching-learning strategy, they will be most meaningful when learners understand the objects and especially when the objects have been well chosen to effectively and accurately explain a specific concept or idea. Learners should choose and explain their metaphors in a manner that makes meaning and sense to other learners. This, therefore, wants facilitators to be careful when selecting these metaphors. Objects have to be familiar to learners or else there is no how learners may relate and see some 'likeness' between objects and the concept being learned. It is for this reason that Glynn and Takahashi (1998) caution us to use carefully chosen analogies because wrong selecting may confuse learners.

Those of us who have used metaphors would agree with Williams (1986) that vivid metaphors have the capability to teach in a way that is not always available with the use of words alone. That is, rather than offer a word-only definition of a new term or concept, the use of a related example using a metaphor can be very helpful to enhance learners' understanding. Indeed, the activity given to the learners demonstrates that learners are thinking 'beings' and when their thinking is directed or assisted, they do it very well. In short, metaphors can promote lively exchange of information anchored in the reasoning, creativeness, conclusion drawing and other attributes that learners possess. Other skills that are promoted through the use of metaphors are listed below.

Skills that can be promoted through using metaphors

Pedagogical use of metaphor helps promote a number of the thinking skills including,

- Creative thinking
- Dialogical thinking
- Critical thinking
- Making conclusions
- Comparisons
- Reflection

Tips for using the metaphor

There are a number of important lessons coming out from the case above. First and foremost, you will realize that when using metaphors as teaching-learning strategies, they are effective when

- Facilitators collect variety of items and pictures for learners to have a number of options. Carefully choose your items based on what you want to achieve through the exercise.
- Facilitators should choose items that are familiar to the learners, foreign items will not work.
- Learners should be given clear instruction of where their choice will eventually lead to, that is, giving reasons for it and describing it.
- The metaphor game is usually effective when you do not have large classes. Alternatively, you may divide learners into small groups to share their ideas. In this case, you need to move around to make your presence, support and guidance explicit.
- Explain how the strategy helps in achieving the objectives of that particular lesson.
- Always provide feedback on learners' work and summarize the critical points of the lesson in a manner that accentuate how the objectives of the lessons have been achieved.
- Get feedback from learners about how they feel about the use of the strategy in class (metaphor) and the skills that they have

developed through the use of this exercise. You may go further by asking them why they believe it is important to have such skills.

Remember there are many other strategies that you may use to develop the thinking skills. In this chapter, examples of the in-basket approach, a word puzzle game and metaphor were given. Remember thinking skills are needed in every learning activity and in practice too. These can also be promoted through out-of-class activities.

An activity

A number of skills were targeted through the exercises given in this chapter. See which ones you believe are more or less important in your situation.

Thinking Skills	Highly needed	Occasionally needed	Not needed	Comments
Critical				
Reflective				
Dialogical				
Adaptive				
Contextual				
Reasoning				
Judgment				
Decision-making				
Selective				

- How important do you believe the thinking skill is in your life?
- Of the strategies that have been presented for teaching thinking skills, which one have you used and how different, if there have been some differences, from the way the facilitators in this book used them?
- In doing the checklist exercise provided, which skill got 'Can do without'? Please provide reasons for your skills
- You may now start thinking about real life situations in which thinking skills are called upon or challenged.

CHAPTER 6
EMOTIONAL AND RELATIONAL SKILLS

Our logical side may help us set goals, but it is our emotional side that provides the passion to persevere through trying times (Jensen, 2008).

Introduction

It is obviously much difficult to separate emotions from learning. Like Jensen (2008) says, a call for holistic learning means that facilitators should acknowledge and consider learners' emotions, feelings, attitudes, and problems. The importance of considering these in our teaching-learning experiences has also been emphasized by Miller (2006), who declares that learning is not limited to the intellect; it is also connected to the emotion, the body and soul. Think, for example, of how learners feel when we discuss their identities, life challenges, experiences and communities. These topics appeal to the hearts or emotions. For example, the influence of emotions to behavior can be immense (Jensen, 2008). Yes, many of us facilitators have experienced situations of learners' undisciplined emotions in our classes. The situation can be really bad and disrupting.

Learners need to be taught skills that will help them to modulate their emotions, that is, to be helped to positively handle emotional situations when they arise and gain attitude necessary to know when they engage in inhumane manner. We have an obligation as facilitators, to teach learners how to regulate their emotions, remembering that an "undisciplined emotion can harm our rational thinking, [and also that] lack of emotion can make for equally flawed thinking" (Jensen, 2008:82).

A number of skills are said to be necessary for relating with other people. These include emotionally intelligence, respect, care, trust and courtesy. All of us need these skills in real life as we relate with others in different environments like homes and workplaces. Naested, Potvin and Waldron (2003:23) underscore the importance of these skills when stating that "whether it is a relationship to one's self, or to the world, the experience of deep connection arises when there is a profound respect, a deep caring and a quality of 'being with' that honors the truth of participants in a relationship". It is obvious that even in classrooms, "a sense of trust, warmth, safety and peer acceptance is critical" (Jensen, 2008: 131).

Relational skills at a glance

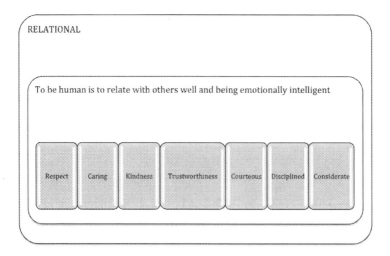

Strategies for teaching relational skills

Working together as a team, for example, cannot be fully achieved without skills such as respect, care, trust and responsibility. What we know, is that in life when an individual relates with others, he or she is expected to do so in a humane and respectful manner.

Emotions and relational skills can be promoted using variety of strategies. In here I present just some few examples.

Observation

Having taught for a long time, I have realized that some time facilitators take for granted the way learners relate during lessons. There are instances where we choose to make it 'none of our business' when some undisciplined emotions in class like some verbal fighting occur. We take comfort in thinking that perhaps the fight is not so open to disturb the class; or it has not even been reported. But really, aren't these occurrences some indications that facilitators are not doing much to help learners know the importance of controlling their emotions? Some learners are simply disrespectful of others' emotions. Are facilitators really responsible for ensuring that learners respect each other? Yes. I believe facilitators should intervene all the time. Ignoring disrespect on the pretext that it does not distract the class, works against the very intention of promoting emotional and relational skills. We need these skills both in the running of our classes as well as for living in our communities.

Those of us who are committed to promoting these skills grab every opportunity to do so. Here is an example.

Case 13: Emotional and relational sample

During one semester, one facilitator had chairs and tables normally short for all learners to sit down. It was a matter of 'first come, first served'. At one time, this well mature learner (mature by age as he was over 40 years) came almost at the same time with a younger learner (in her early 20s). They ran for the remaining chair. The younger one was fast, so she grabbed it first. The mature learner used his physical strength to push the younger one down, took the chair away and made himself comfortable on it. The facilitator watched this incident and decided to intervene. Other learners were also watching.

Before teaching, she said, 'there are some very valuable personality traits that we should not forget anywhere; in classrooms, in the street, churches, workplaces and homes, just everywhere. One of these is respect for others or 'botho'.

∫

In the Setswana culture (Botswana), *botho* means humane behavior. It gives a concept of a person who has a well-rounded character, who is well mannered/courteous/disciplined. It disapproves of anti-social, disgraceful and inhuman behaviors (Republic of Botswana, Presidential Task Force, 1997).

∫

The facilitator was quite aware that the majority of learners understood what she actually meant by '*botho*'. Just by mentioning '*botho*', learners who were well socialized to understand the impact of a statement such as 'you lack *botho*' could read the facilitator's concern. She explained that most bad behaviors start small, for example, as a bad look at someone, teasing, using profane language and just pushing others around. She implored learners to refrain from these behaviors and have '*botho*'.

Like it has already mentioned, to teach about *botho* is to emphasize respect for each other. This principle when applied to the classroom situations addresses closely the nitty-gritties of classroom relationships such as self-discipline, harmonious exchange of information and care about each other's feelings. When examined from a personal perspective, the philosophy of *botho* helps to develop a caring and trusting family member. When we look at it from the community point of view, the community is blessed to have members with *botho* because they respect each other and are loyal to each other. In a nation, citizens with '*botho*' can help the country to develop by reducing the level of crime, cheating and untrustworthiness. If classrooms instill in learners the need to have *botho*, then, families, communities and nations will be assured of members who value their relationship with others.

Case 14: Using the observation strategy to teach relational skills

Based on the discussion of the need to relate well to each other, and the case that was used to demonstrate the need for '*botho*', the facilitator gave learners the following activity.

> The facilitator said, 'for the next lesson, I want all of you to go to social places like shopping centers, streets, traditional meeting places and other schools. You are going to observe behaviors that we can associate with '*botho*' in these places'. Stay in the

chosen location for 30-minutes to one hour and see what you can observe.

Learners had their reflective journals in which they were asked to capture at least three scenes that they thought provided teachable moments, that is, situations that attracted their attention. They were asked to describe these situations as rich as possible and come and share with classmates.

Analyzing Case 14

This assignment has a number of positive aspects in relation to learning about the behaviors or ways in which people relate or interact with one another. Importantly,

- To ask learners to observe behaviors in authentic settings is to bring them as close to reality as possible. Experience has taught us that values such as *botho* are learned well if observed in natural settings in which they come spontaneously and are not pretended.
- Learning is fun as it is self-directed and free from classroom rules.
- Leaners may come across something surprising, the unexpected and other real dynamics of people's behaviors. This gives them a chance to reflect on their own behaviors especially when they think they are not watched. Learners are likely to develop some desire to live in a way that is congruent to what they observe to be 'good' behavior.

Through this activity, the facilitator demonstrates to her learners that

- Our actions give meaning to what we learn. Learners, through observing, understand the nuances or dynamics of what it takes to behave in a socially appropriate manner. In reporting what they observed, they reflected on a number of behaviors and attitudes associated with *botho* (care, respect, tolerance, shy, appreciation, humorous, honesty, empathy, genuine and love).
- Learning becomes much more immediate when you experiment with it. This is very true because many learners reported having learned so much within a very short period of time. Although the facilitator encouraged them to choose one place, some reported having observed in more than one place because it was fun for them to observe people who were not aware that they were being observed.

Skilled developed through Case 14: Observation

Skills	Description as is in the case
Decision-making	The activity expects learners to decide where they go for observation. This is not just a simply task. They should make informed decisions or else their time will be wasted observing a place which yields very little for them to be informative.
Making judgment	Learners do not report anything and everything they observe, they select. Selection is a process of making judgment, this means, being able to realize when they make good points and when they miss a point.

Independence/self-directedness	Although this activity may be done in groups, in this case, it was not. A learner worked on his or her own. This helps in developing learner's self-directedness or independence skills.
Confidentiality	When they observe, there may be situations where they meet people they know or even those that they do not know. Really, learners are not supposed to talk about the identities of the people they observe but their behaviors. So, let them discuss targeted behaviors and not 'individuals per se' who display such a behavior.
Respect	Learners learn to respect people's privacy. That is, during observation, they cannot intervene even where they may be tempted to do so because permission to observe has not been granted.

Tips for using the observation strategy in real life settings outside classrooms

- Carefully choose places on the basis of what they can offer as teaching-learning sites. Choose them only if they can give meaning to the topic of discussion and provide learners with more enlightenment to a specific topic.
- Consider the proximity of places to visit to the school. The activity should not put extra demand on the learners, for example, in terms of transport and food.
- Take all precautions to ensure learners' safety.
- Before learners go out to observe, give them enough background knowledge to do the observation well, for example, describe the strategy to the leaners and explain why you believe such strategy is suitable for the exercise at hand.

- Explain how the strategy will help in achieving the objectives of that particular lesson.
- Make clear to the learners what will make the strategy work for them (what you expect learners to do).
- During presentation, always provide feedback on the presentations and summarize the critical points of the lesson in a manner that accentuate how the objectives of the lessons have been achieved.
- Get feedback from learners about how they feel about the use of the strategy in class (observation) and its benefits outside class.

Remember, there are many other strategies that may be used to develop the relational or emotional skills. These include debate, guest lecturing, home visits, dramatization or role-play, research or field trip. An example of how to use dramatization follows.

Dramatization

Facilitators at times want their learners to be able to display their emotions and talk about how such emotions help them in life. In my classes, I usually ask learners to role-play or act out some situations from their life situations. An example is given below.

First, I presented a stimulus that follows for them to start thinking of the play.

Case 15: Emotions displayed

> The man who skipped the queue returned the insult with even more serious 'profane' language. The speed within which the man at the back came and grabbed

the other man with clothes was amazing. The fight started. During their fight, the man who was accused of skipping the queue pushed his opponent against the wall and seriously bruised his face. The police officers were called in and the two men were apprehended. It was then when the policy arrested them that we learned that the man was actually not skipping. He had asked someone to hold the queue for him.

I explained to my learners that I had witnessed a fight at the post office. People were in a long queue. Apparently someone came and proceeded straight to be served. One of the people at the back end of the queue who, at that time, was already impatient of long waiting

The case was presented specifically to illustrate the concept of 'emotionally intelligence'. Major (2008) defines emotional intelligence as the ability to deal peacefully with anger, insults, hurt and disappointments.

The learners were given a group activity to analyze the scenario. Their task was to list 'the intelligent' and the 'non-intelligent' actions and give reasons for their listing. Thereafter, learners shared their responses.

Furthermore, learners were asked to recount instances they have witnessed of similar manner. After being well vested on the topic of discussion, that is, emotional intelligence, they developed a role-play. It was to be a dyadic situation in which the behavior was displayed and a means to correct that behavior illustrated too, even if it means the intervention would not work as intended.

Analyzing the Case

When it came to the actual act of dramatizing, it was superb. It was clear that learners thought seriously about their plays. They displayed important conflict resolution skills that could help save 'ugly' situations like the one presented in the Case 15. Most groups went through their drama well with actions anchored in the group's thinking. This was obvious in situations where the actor seemed not to do what the group expected, you could notice some signs of disapproval or hear some advices from group members.

Of all groups, one drama that particular interested me was a case in the traditional Setswana court, called a 'kgotla'.

A kgotla is a public meeting, community council or traditional law court, especially in villages of Botswana, usually referred to as a customary court. It is usually headed by the village chief or headman, and community decisions are always arrived at by consensus. Anyone at all is allowed to speak, and no one may interrupt while someone is giving his or her views (http://en.wikipedia.org/wiki/Kgotla).

Case 16: Acting out emotions

A boy who has fled his parent's home to live in the street was brought before the traditional court to be disciplined for stealing from someone's car. He broke the window after realizing that there was a bag of groceries in the back seat. Unfortunately for him, the owner came in good time to find him and called the police.

Before the police came, the boy was disciplined by the 'mob' court (people who saw him stealing). He was now facing another court discipline. The boy felt the mob had done the punishment and he should be left alone. He decided not to listen to anyone but just scream whenever asked questions. It was irritating to those who were to discipline him. So, they decided that he should be whipped regardless of refusing to talk. The boy screamed more. Then suddenly an old man of 80 years stood up and said,

'See, all eyes are on you! Even your own eyes are on you. We want to help you, not you helping us.

[The boy wanted to open up his mouth to scream again, as he has being doing].

The old man continued, 'See all eyes are on you! I saw your teeth when you opened your mouth. What happened to them! Crude life, no water to wash them, no house to sleep. Hmm, tough life, no tooth brush, no toothpaste and no manners. Oh crude life indeed! Do you know that very soon you will have no life? Your teeth are rotten with worms that have now started eating you alive. Soon, you will have no life. Why are you doing this to yourself? You need help and we want to help you.

[There was fear in the boy's face, perhaps he believed the worms have started 'eating' his flesh].

The boy eventually said, 'Ok, I need some help?' What help? The old man asked. 'I don't know, the boy said. The old man said, 'I think I have a good idea for you, Let's go'.

[The play ended with the old man and young boy going away].

For me, it is not the logic of the old man's argument but how he has managed to save a situation that had the potential to worsen. The boy was already angry that the mob had done its part and he was now going to be disciplined by the 'kgotla' people. The boy was just about to be whipped or taken to prison for the one offense that the mob disciplined him for. All these made him more 'mad'. His behavior was off-hands until the old man thought and saved the situation. The old man was not 'fed up' with the boy like others. He wanted to help and so he became patience and careful in dealing with the boy. The end result is gain for all.

Benefits for using dramatization

The reasons for using roleplaying are many and sound. First, it brings us closer to reality with well-thought-of actions. Also,

- It is fun to use. More than other things, it allows learners to be excited as they watch how their thoughts turn into actions. Acting is a moment that allows learners to reflect, analyze and question their thinking.

- It allows learners to picture themselves in the situation being acted and in one way or the other, it teaches new behavior.
- It gives learners chance to exercise their decision-making skills as they discuss and decide the roles to take and how such roles are to be played.
- Learners rediscover themselves or assess their previous behaviors in the light of their drama.
- It develops learners' self-confidence as they see themselves making some important decisions on what to act and how to act it. Taking part in the drama is itself rewarding. It makes them happy to see that others trust and appreciate their roles.
- In some cases like in Case 16, dramatization appeals to the learners' sympathy to people in difficult situations.

Tips for using role play/dramatization

- Roles to be clearly defined—Actions to be explained clearly and thought out in advance before playing. This gives learners chance to select who they believe best suit the roles. Learners sometimes volunteer to play these roles.
- Explain clearly the type of role-playing you want learners to engage in. You may give example or a stimulus like in the case we just explored.
- Don't assume that learners understand how to role-play. Describe this strategy to the leaners and explain why you believe such strategy is suitable for the lesson being taught.
- Explain how the strategy helps in achieving the objectives of that particular lesson.
- Make clear to the learners what will make the strategy work for them (what you expect learners to do).
- Ensure that the activity is clearly explained and everything to make it successful has been made available to the learners.

- During presentation, comment and provide feedback on learners' presentation and summarize the critical points of the lesson in a manner that accentuate how the objectives of the lessons have been achieved.
- Get feedback from learners about how they feel about the use of the strategy in class and its benefits outside class.

The last strategy that I want to present as effective in developing emotional and relational skills is debate.

Debate as a pedagogical strategy for developing emotional or relational skills

It has already been said that learners learn more when they have fun in learning. Debate does not only bring fun but engages learners all the time. It brings learners close to experiencing the real argument and calls for their thinking and actions. Thinking and actions are the two most important aspects that drive effective learning for most of us. The case that follows indicates that from a debating session, leaners usually emerge with important skills.

Case 17: Debate as a teaching-learning strategy

> In the discussion of child poverty/delinquency, I made a statement that perhaps parents should be blamed. At that time, I had a feeling that poverty was a result of lack of hard work by parents, and, delinquency indicates a child's reactions to what he or she did not like about his or her parents. I no longer feel this way. There are many factors leading to this situation. For example, the rich people are sponges that absorb all the riches and use the poor to accumulate more

wealth. See, the type of work the poor do and the salaries they get. My heart tells me that those children from the poor families should resist working for the rich, let them get education and think smart about ways of breaking free from poverty. The other side of my thinking says this is not possible. Where do the poor get money because education these days is bought? Now, these days I am tempted to brush away any thinking about how the poor can be helped. My mind runs from yes, they may be helped, to some disagreement that there is no how that they can be free of this situation. 'What do you think?'

With this background, I asked the learners to go into 2 groups. It was a small class so each group was less than ten. I gave learners some ten minutes to talk freely about the topic or subject of discussion to be sure they understand the gist of the discussion. They were further asked to consider the two sides of the discussion as presented in the introduction. Finally, they were to make decisions, that is, the two groups agreed on which group to take each of the two perspectives, 'Yes, poverty can be eradicated' or 'No, it's there to stay with us'. Learners were given 30 minutes to prepare for their 15 minutes debate.

The main goals for giving learners a debating activity was

- To see how learners express their feelings towards the poor— for example, in their debate, learners were asked to describe how they feel about the problem of poverty and to further describe the reasons for their feelings.
- To see how learners perceive and react to different points of view—for example, 'Yes, poverty can be eradicated and No, it's here to stay with us'. It will also be interesting to see the

attitudes with which learners present their argument, for example, whether there is a sense of caring about the situation of others or not? Do they display 'it's their problem not mine' attitude?

- To see how best learners can manage their emotions or impulse when challenged by others—for example, can they argue, disagree in a constructive manner? Learners who are emotionally intelligence enjoy their learning because they think through what is being said; learn from others' criticisms in a non-offensive manner.

- One of the greatest advantages of debate is that it helps learners to acknowledge that in life people are free to express their opinions.

In other word, the facilitator here was more interested in seeing how compassionate, caring and emotional intelligence are displayed.

Analyzing the Case

What learners are taught through the debate activity has a direct relationship with life as experienced by real people outside the classroom. The plight of the poor is well known to all of us, together with the different theories and line of thoughts that try to explain this situation, some helpful and some not. It is, therefore, important that a situation like this be presented to learners to get their perspective on it. Like Johnson and Johnson (2009) say, "in order to make sense of the world, individuals need to share their perceptions and reactions with other people and find out whether or not other people perceive and react similarly" (p. 11). The exercise indeed brought different perspectives from the learners' point of view about the situation of the poor.

In the Case discussed by the learners, a number of skills were nurtured including

- Communication—learners communicate throughout the process of planning and acting out their debates. In the process, the interpersonal communication skills and conflict resolution are exercised.
- Debate contributes strongly to learners' acquisition of critical skills, for example, many ideas are brought up as learners prepare for their debates and what they do is to make the most brilliant decision of what to include and what to leave out. It is a way of judging the meaningfulness and worth of ideas.
- There is no doubt that learners' confidence and feeling of empowerment are developed as they hear and see themselves reasoning and arguing their point of view against those of their colleagues. They feel so fulfilled when they see that they contribute in a way appreciated not only by themselves but others.
- As learners debate, they are in the process of acquiring important public speaking skills. Debate can help learners who otherwise would be intimidated to talk in front of people to gain confidence of doing so.
- People who engage in debate develop good listening skills; they listen to others so that when they follow up what has been said, it demonstrates logic and good listening skills.

Tips for using the debate as a learning strategy

- Give learners enough background to engage in debate. Debate may be directed as it was in Case 17. It can start with a short discussion of the topic, a reading directed to the topic to be discussed or a short lecture on the topic. This is to give learners the background and understanding of what the debate is all about.

- Describe this strategy to the leaners and explain why you believe it is suitable for the exercise at hand.
- Explain how the strategy helps in achieving the objectives of that particular lesson.
- Make clear to the learners what will make the strategy work for them (what you expect learners to do), for example, during the debate, learners have to listen carefully to others, summarize the critical points and it is after this that they can make intelligent contributions or argument.
- Encourage learners to be open-minded as they are expected to see the problem from the two perspectives before they can decide to support or take sides.
- Select two or four learners to take note of the critical points being raised by each team. These will be used at the end for summary or to lead questions and further discussions.
- Always provide feedback on learners' presentation and summarize the critical points of the lesson in a manner that accentuate how the objectives of the lessons have been achieved.
- Get feedback from learners about how they feel about the use of the strategy in class and its benefits outside class.

An activity

Here is an activity to help you reflect on the skills that we explored in this chapter.

- Why is it necessary that we build strong relationships in and outside our classrooms?
- What do you think happens when some learners feel unaccepted by others learners?
- How best can you integrate emotions into the learning process?
- Some undesirable behavior may occur on the side of your learners regardless of teaching them how to use their emotions in a productive manner. How best will you use a lesson on 'emotional intelligence' to underscore the importance of good behavior?

CHAPTER 7
ESSENTIALS OF PRACTICAL SKIILS

Learning becomes a true asset if what happens in institutions is never cosmetic or merely symbolic; it must be capable of being extended and applied to the social and political conditions present outside its classroom walls (Searle, 1981).

Introduction

This chapter explores strategies that can engage learners with the worlds outside their classrooms or schools. These are the real worlds where they will eventually apply lessons gained in classrooms. If learners are given learning tasks that can connect them to the communities, they will appreciate community as a learning space. Oblinger (2006), for example, defines community as a powerful context of learning. When learners learn within this rich context, their expectations of what it is like to work are shaped by reality rather than theories.

Practical skills at a glance

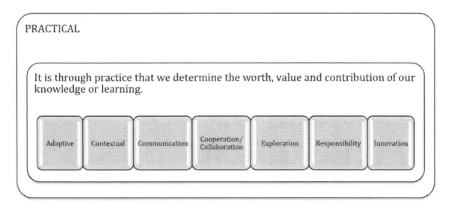

Developing practical skills

Practical skills can be developed using a number of strategies. In here, I give some few examples.

The outreach strategies

Practical skills are explained here as skills that one can apply to perform tasks. These are developed both through classroom teaching and application. The discussion here focuses on the latter:—that is, developing them through application, specifically, the outreach activities. Outreach means that learners reach out to people in contexts other than their classrooms. They can visit industries, homes, churches and other places that will provide rich learning.

A number of strategies can be employed to take learners outside the classrooms. These include field trips, home visits and voluntarism.

Field trip

Filed-work means that facilitators and learners make connections with people outside the school environments. These may be workplaces, homes, churches and other organizations. In applying their knowledge in these environments, learners see the value of their learning. When their ideas or knowledge work, they can right away see how what they learn is useful and get motivated to continue to learn. A case is presented below as an example.

Case18: Sample field-based learning

In her course, 'Entrepreneurial Skills Development', the facilitator decided to take her learners out on a field trip to observe a small business owned by a youth. She took them to a farm.

This Dairy House Farm started production in 2002 with the aim of producing both fresh and sour or curdled milk (*Madila*). The sour milk is made using traditional utensils like plastic bag, natural sunbeam and cooling system made from a wooden shelter. There are modern machines such as milking machines, milk tubes attached to the cow's udder. These are used to produce enough milk to convert the practice into commercial industry.

The sales of fresh milk and *sour milk* are tracked through the use of an ICT gadget, the computer. This family uses Internet and media such as *Farmers' Digest* to identify cows that can produce more milk. The benefits of the farm to the community are multifolds. It hires people from the village in which it is located and this is a rural place. This project also contributes directly to community members not working in the farm. They are given liquid whey for free and the product is useful in a number of ways. It can be used to cook sour meal (sorghum or porridge). Overall, the product is highly nutritious and can reduce malnutrition among children (Excerpt from Garegae, 2011, in Lekoko & Semali (Eds.)

In this farm, there are so many things to interest the learners. Some learners may be interested in knowing about the milking process. Others may be fascinated by the amount of milk coming from a single cow and wanting to know what makes that cow to produce that much milk. Still, others may like a different life, a farm life as it differs from life in town. Technology such as computers and those used to milk the cow may constitute another line of interest for some learners. While all these may be of interest to an entrepreneur, a skillful facilitator should know exactly what he or she is looking for on a trip like this one. Thus, directed field experience is very important.

Directed field experience implies that facilitator has made it clear to the learner what they are to observe and capture in their field learning journals. Not everything but enough to indicate that the trip has been justified. For example, in Case 18 that we just explored, learners were specifically asked to inquire about marketing and management strategies. Other observations should come in to support this focus.

The field trip itself is rich with information. Learners learn by direct observation, seeing, feeling, tasting and doing these constitute the richness of learning.

As Case 18 illustrates, it is the process of planning for the field trip that helps

- To instill the spirit of commitment on the part of learners and facilitators.
- Help build strong communication skills—planners or organizers communicate regularly about their plans and this is a way of promoting these skills.
- It helps build cooperation and collaboration among those involved in the trip.
- Good planning has actually ensured that every learner is actively involved as each was given a role to play, individually and as a member of the team.

Skills developed through fieldtrip

The field trip can be used to develop a number of skills including the following;

- Observation—there is so much to observe in the field and learners learn to focus, select the best, the relevant or meaningful.
- Research—Field trip requires learners to search for knowledge, they enter the field with an open mind to learn, apply what they know, to confirm, refute or strengthen theories. They may even develop new theories as a result of having interacted with the natural environments.
- Reflecting—What is observed in the field prompts learners to reflect on what has been learned, on their own lives or on their assumptions. It is this reflection that opens up for new learning.

- Responsibility—Field trip comes with some defined responsibilities on the part of learners. The facilitator directs activities and each learner has some responsibility to do.
- Networking—To reach out to others outside the school environments means to network. Learners exercise their cooperation and collaboration skills as they plan for and engage in their field trips.

Tips for using field trip as a learning strategy

- In planning the field trip, facilitators should always consider the richness of the field, that it, it can arouse something that has not been on the plan. Facilitators, therefore, should be aware of what to allow in and what should be kept out.
- The process of planning for field is just as important as the time of being in the trip. If you really want to know if your field trip is successful, wait until you get to the field. The field is dynamic and spontaneous. There may be so many interesting things to learn from and the facilitator has a duty to direct learners to choose the most appropriate as determined by the objective of the lesson and the time available for learners to be in the field.
- Planning must be thoroughly done before going for field trip. Plan strategically. This means fully weighing the advantages and disadvantages of going out against teaching that topic in class, if possible. To construct a realistic plan, gather all important information. The goal is to get a good idea of what can make the field trip fail or succeed.
- It is not enough just to think of taking learners out. This comes with some challenges. As Case 18 indicates, resources are needed. The trip comes with all kinds of costs—emotional, financial, spiritual and others. These have to be thought of

and cannot be allowed to take facilitators and learners by surprise.

- Assemble a small planning group of learners who can commit their time and credibility to plan for the outreach activity. Most importantly, the facilitator should work hand-in-hand with this group.
- Give each member of the planning smaller tasks to do, for different substantive areas of the field trip, for example, resources, communication, time planning and others.
- Encourage them to report their progress to the class (they may be given 5-10 minutes at the beginning or end of class to give feedback). This helps to keep other learners on track of the progress and planners also get important feedback and advice from the class. The whole class becomes part of the planning.
- Often hold feedback sessions with the planning team in which each member reports on a task given and individual's tasks are put together to see the group's progress. This leads to follow-ups where necessary and new tasks set if needed.
- At the end of the trip, facilitators always bring learners back together in a classroom atmosphere to reflect on their experiences of the trip and what they have learned. Always develop guiding questions to lead in the sharing of experiences.
- Always provide feedback on learners' presentation and summarize the critical points of their presentation in a manner that accentuate how the objectives of the lessons have been achieved.

Field placements/Internship

It is customary that many institutions provide learners with field experiences in a form of practical internship. Few will doubt the merit of this supervised practice. Not all courses or programs call for field attachment or internship. An example of a course that demands a field internship learning activity is presented below.

Case 19: Sample Internship

> Over the past three years I have been teaching a course aimed at exposing learners, experientially or practically, to different ways of facilitating in an adult learning program. Students entering this course have been exposed (in an earlier course) to the literature on adult teaching/learning methods. They are full time extension officers working in such diverse contexts as prisons, community development, social work, health, consumer education, wild life, transport and communication. Learners are to be attached outside the formal school environments to observe and practice how adult teaching methods are applied.

Some observations from Case 19

Interships are by nature very difficult to organise. Very often, problems or challenges keep surfacing even in cases where careful planning was done. Here are some few examples of what happened in this particular internship (Case 19).

> One learner could not get accommodation where he was attached. He was told no one was willing to share a house with him. Instead of six weeks of internship he spent only three because he took time organizing his own accommodation.

Another learner got accommodation and found that the class teacher was not willing to let him teach as she was preparing her students for examination. She was drilling her students using past examination papers and did not want this process to be interrupted.

The third learner was turned down by the head teacher who was absent when arrangements to accommodate her were made. She had bad experience with previous students of this particular college/university. She claimed they misbehaved and were not serious. She had decided not to ever take anyone from this particular university. A placement was found for her two weeks before the end of the internship.

While there are rewards associated with doing an internship, it is clear on the other hand that internship can give some 'headaches'. Issues of being accepted in the field are proving to be complex as in Case 19. For example, learners who do not carry themselves well, can leave a bad trail for those that are to come. Furthermore, we are made aware of contingency matters. Some times, you may have planned on time but just at the last moment, the plans change. What is important is to be always on the look out for eventualities like the ones that happened in Case 19. The suggested framework for doing internship does not imply that learners and facilitators will not face some challenges, it at least ensures good planning. It is a framework that is suitable in situations where learners are responsible for finding their hosts, working hand-in-hand with their facilitators.

Tips for using internship as a learning strategy

Suggestions that are made here focus on resources, relationship and institutional support.

Support Features

These include institutional support, reputation and field receptivity.

Institutional support refers to how the institution supports learners on field practice. For instance, to afford learners the needed regular and prolonged stay in the host, resources should be made available (transport, lodging, food and equipment are to be made available). This type of engagement cannot be done without the financial and other resources.

Institutional reputation: The institution sending learners out should have a long and favorable reputation with the hosts. This reputation aids field receptivity.

Field receptivity: A number of organizations should be willing to host diversity of interests and specialization of learners. Since participation by host is voluntary, each prospective host must be persuaded of the benefits to be derived from participating in the activity.

Student Characteristics

Successful placement is also a result of the type of learners who go to the field; their motivation, commitment and authority.

Student motivation: In this case, students are responsible for selecting and procuring their field placement with minimal supervision from the course facilitators. Motivation to engage in this activity will sustain them and help them go through this process successfully.

Student authority: Because the learners are responsible for procuring their own sites, they must persuade potential hosts on the basis of their 'professional expertise'. In other words, in soliciting placement, learners must be viewed as professionals on their own rights. Their level of preparedness and expertise constitute this authority.

Curricula Features

The success of which depends on the working together of the learners and facilitators. There has to be some mutual understanding of the roles to be played by each one, for example, the facilitator respects learner's choices—changes are mutually agreed upon by the learner and facilitator. Learners should be open and free to share their experiences with the facilitator. Self-evaluation (positive and negative) is encouraged as a positive method of self-appraisal.

Planning entails developing tentative plans of what learners are expected to do in the field and what will make this experience successful, like, the availability of transport and equipment and access to the materials needed. Prior knowledge that learners bring to the activity and the characteristics of the learners are to be taken into consideration too. Also, guidelines are developed for writing reflective journals and the final report. Learners begin field work only when the facilitators are convinced that the activity has been well planned for.

Fieldwork: Learners put their plans in action. They also keep a reflective journal that they share with the facilitator and colleagues. They attend weekly one-hour debriefing session that serves as a way to monitor progress and guide future actions. Students are encouraged to suggest discussion topics for this meeting. Their reflective journals are also major sources of discussion topics. This period takes no more than six weeks, at the end of which, each student and/or team submits a written report.

Placements come in different forms. Case 19 illustrates a situation where learners are expected to find their own hosts. We are also used to situations where students are placed without much input from them.

Placement helps in developing important skills such as

- Consultation
- Cooperation/collaboration
- Communication
- Inquiring
- Responsibility
- Research
- Independence
- Professionalism
- Leadership

Home visits

As the name implies, learners are sent to the homes and communities to learn with and from them.

Case 20: Sample home visit learning

Learners were asked to do some home visits. This time, they were going to share or make families aware and be accustomed to using emergency numbers and services when need be. Before sharing with families, learners were to tell families a story (as an advance organizer) that would help families see the need for knowing some of these emergency numbers and services. Learners started with stories such as the ones illustrated below.

 Why do certain things happen to us?

One day, in the dark rainy night, I was attacked by two men. I was walking home from late studying in the library. I could feel some chill when they approached but a small voice inside me told me to just walk and they would pass. I kept walking but was uneasy and avoided to keep looking back at them. I have no idea when they caught up with me because what I remember is that I was beaten so hard that I could not move. I think they left me when satisfied, but with what? I don't know. They seemed to enjoy kicking me and punching me without uttering a single word.

They did not try to rob me. I still had my cellphone after they left me in the rain. I panicked at the thought of them coming back for more punching. I took my phone from my pocket. I did not know any emergency number. I tried calling my home, no one answered and I learned the phone was not working as the power was cut off by a thunderstorm. So, I laid there helpless.

Many learners started with a short story like the one above. This was used to trigger discussion and to illustrate the type of emergency situations one may find himself or herself in. After the story was shared, some discussions around it started as a way to hear the initial reactions by the family members to a situation like the one shared. Some families who have experienced similar situations were expected to share their experiences too. Individuals too were free to share stories that happened to them or those that they knew happened to some people. The discussion was to be kept short as it was meant to pave way to sharing and learning emergency numbers and services and how to use them. When family members shared stories and commented on them, learners got a sense of what their listeners thought about these numbers. For example, after this task, many learners reported that some families had some confused or misguided understanding about the use of emergency numbers. A common confusion was to see police officers and cars as bringing trouble to the family or viewing them as irresponsive to calls, therefore, anything that had to do with the police was avoided.

This activity taught about emergency numbers such;

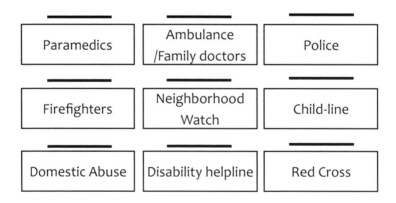

Paramedics	Ambulance /Family doctors	Police
Firefighters	Neighborhood Watch	Child-line
Domestic Abuse	Disability helpline	Red Cross

Analysis of the Case

As children practice calling these emergency numbers using toy phones, it gives them the 'how-to' skills and instills in them the need to consider using them seriously whenever the need arises. Careful use of these numbers give a signal that other important guideposts like road signs, emergency vehicles like ambulance and police may be respected too. In the activity, learners and family members are familiarized with these numbers so that when they are confronted with real life situations of using them, they do not encounter much problem.

The possibility of families cooperating with schools on the use of emergency numbers is high as they are both serious about the safety of children. Learners engage in doing this type of homework learn a great deal of family values. They also have an opportunity to contribute to the family. Where they see that families' belief may stand in their way of using the emergency numbers, for example, in the case of the myths about the police, they take this opportunity to dispel such myths. Above all other else, both learners and family members learn to work together, to cooperate, share ideas and learn together. From this process of families working with learners, other important skills of communication, consultation, trust and reasoning are promoted.

 Some practical tips for using home visits

- Schedule home visits on time to allow learners to prepare and plan for them. They have to consult homes they are to visit and negotiate their entry into these homes. Random visits should not be allowed as learners have to visit only those homes that have given them permission. They should always get permission from families.

- Home visit is done to achieve some specified objectives. These objectives come from the contents to be covered and as indicated in the course outline. It should not come as an add-on just to keep learners away from the classrooms and provide a breakaway for the facilitator to do something else.
- The first visit to the homes by learners for making appointments is the first impression the family will make about these learners. Learners should treat it with care and respect for the families and present themselves with some authority that will convince the family that indeed there is something worth learning from them.
- Learners should always explain the purpose of their visits and the amount of time that the activity will require. They should mutually agree with families on the actual time for visiting.
- A home visit may be done by a single learner, or in pairs or groups. Really, I prefer single or dyad to avoid crowding the family.
- The seriousness and commitment demonstrated by the learners during the home visits will go a long way to develop a strong working relationship of the school and community.
- Facilitators should advise their learners that when a family refuses them permission to share with it, they should withdraw with respect and move to the next one. Very few families will refuse to give learners this opportunity unless there is an unpleasant history behind their refusal.
- Learners should be careful and observant not to approach homes in difficult situations like mourning.
- Visiting homes is an ideal time for getting to know family values and building relationship with people in the community. Learners should, therefore, be prepared for it.

Guest lecturing

Guest lecturing may be an answer to some practical questions that get to be asked and never get answered by regular class facilitator within the four walls of the classrooms. Guest lecturing is closely related to activities where learners visit an organization to be given a short lecture about what happens in that particular organization. The following case gives an example of when and how to use a guest lecturer.

Case 21: Sample situation for guest lecturing

I am running a 3-week long training workshop on 'professionalism'. We are now in a topic 'What make a professional'. We discussed the characteristics of a professional but still something is missing. I know very little about professionals in different settings because I just got my first job after my undergraduate degree. I cannot make learners to be aware of professionals in different settings. I decided to call 3 guest lecturers to talk about professionalism in their different settings. I did this because I wanted learners to understand that being a professional is shaped by many factors, including the environment in which one practices.

∫

I invited three guest lecturers. One was from Prison Department. Another person was from a Bank while the third one was from the Farmer Association.

∫

Analysis of the case

It was a 2-hour lesson, so the three guest lecturers came at the same time and each presented for 20 minutes. The lectures were very helpful. They provided richer accounts of 'real professionalism' in their different worlds. Definitely, a person from the Bank had a different experience of a professional when compared to that from the farming environment. One common conclusion reached through these presentations was that all professionals had general common traits, including: knowledge and skills of the profession, commitment to self-improvement, service orientation, pride in the profession, professional relationship with client, creativity and innovation, conscience and trustworthiness, accountability for his or her work, ethically sound decision making and leadership (Hill, 2000).

At the end of the presentation, I was convinced that the guest lecturers were persuasive enough in asking learners to visit their places of work to observe and compare what they said with what was happening in their real worlds of work. In other word, they agreed that guest lecturing could not illustrate succinctly what happened but at least it gave real personal experiences of what was believed to be happening in each work environment. However, what is important is that through this strategy, learners are able to appreciate the importance of teamwork between schools and workplaces. In situations where learners are given the responsibility to look for guest lecturers, their consultation, communication and interdisciplinary skills are nurtured.

Tips for using guest lecturing as a learning strategy

- Recruit the right kind of a person for guest lecturing

- Give the person a specific topic to cover—this is important because my experience with guest lecturers is that many of them have a lot to share and actually need some boundaries.
- Provide the necessary support and guidance, for example, class time, equipment available, characteristics of your learners.
- Ask the guest lecturer what his or her expectations are when accepting the invitation.
- Let learners know about the person's visit and credibility to serve as a guest lecturer.

An activity

As we come to the conclusion of practical skills, you may like to do the following activity as a reminder of some of these skills we explored in this chapter.

Practical Skills	Highly needed	Occasionally needed	Not needed	Comments
Contextual				
Adaptive				
Creative				
Innovative				
Communication				
Responsible				
Collaborative				
Planning				
Thinking				

- Go over the activity and see which skills you checked 'not needed' and provide cases for supporting your claim.
- What constraints do you usually encounter in doing outreach activities?

CHAPTER 8
LEVERAGING COOPERATION AND COLLABORATION SKILLS

Education should give students a sense of solidarity and community with others, locally, nationally and globally so that they can learn to work cooperatively with others and understand how their actions affect them (Osborne, 1991).

Introduction

This chapter focuses on building cooperation or collaboration, the skills needed by all of us. These days, you will agree with me that there is no single problem that can effectively be dealt with without calling for more than one person present at the discussion table. This makes cooperation and collaboration skills absolutely essential both in and outside formal learning environments. Panitz (1997) as cited in Muijs and Reynolds (2005) defines collaboration learning as a philosophy of personal responsibility and respect and sees cooperation as learning that encompasses all kinds of group work. However, in our learning environments, these skills can be promoted in different forms. We can have a whole class project, a small group or dyad learning tasks. All what we want is for all learners involved to understand the value of cooperation and working collaboratively with others. We all need these skills, because with them we can work as teams, partners and keep together as community of learners.

People do not live as isolates. In respect of this communal living, Mbiti (1988), from an African perspective, reminds us that "an individual does not and cannot exist alone except corporately, he is simply part of the whole, that is, "I am human because I belong, I participate, and I share" (p. 26). Elsewhere in India, Ghandi expressed this fundamental social living ethos when he said, 'the good of the individual is contained in the good of the community' (cited in Stone, 1996). Taken together, these authors prompt all of us to see the importance of cooperative and collaborative skills. Facilitators cannot leave the development of these skills to 'chance'. They are accountable and well positioned to ensure their development.

Cooperation/Collaboration skills at a glance

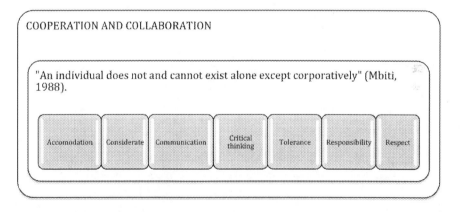

COOPERATION AND COLLABORATION

"An individual does not and cannot exist alone except corporatively" (Mbiti, 1988).

| Accomodation | Considerate | Communication | Critical thinking | Tolerance | Responsibility | Respect |

Strategies for promoting cooperation and collaboration skills

There are a number of strategies that one can use to develop skills for cooperating and collaborating with others well. They include group work, peer teaching, home visits and other fieldwork approaches.

Group work

Group work teaches group living skills. All of us are accustomed to this type of living in all walks of our lives—in our homes, communities and work environments. However, this does not make facilitators assume that all learners have group living skills such as being able to cooperate or collaborate with others. Some fall short of these skills, thus, they need to be taught.

Various group work activities can be given. Below I give an example.

Case 22: Sample group work t activities

In groups of 4 or 5, learners were asked to go and research on a topic of their interest related to philosophies of teaching and learning in adult education. Each member of the team was to be given a task to work on, for example, if learners decided to research on 'The applicability of Maslow's Hierarchy of Needs' to the world of teaching and learning, then they would divide themselves according to levels/hierarchy of needs and each research on it. Each person was then expected to present his or her findings. One requirement of this group work was that a group should meet with another group doing similar topic, if available. This would ensure sharing information and helping each other to cross check the accuracy of their information. It was believed that as they shared information, they would learn from each other. When they finished the project, they were to present in class. Their presentation was to be well-organized.

A case was reported of a group that failed to complete the project. When the report reached the facilitator's desk, there was no hope of resuscitating it because of the nature of disagreement that went on. The facilitator, by deciding to use this case in class, understood the importance of cooperation and collaboration skills. She presented it as a hypothetical case because she wanted to hide the identities of the learners involved.

Presentation of the case to class

The facilitator presented the case to the class to analyze it. This is a way of helping them build, analyze and appreciate why cooperation and being responsible cannot be traded off for opposite behaviors in projects that call for them.

In presenting the case to the class, the facilitator explained the incident.

 It was a group of four - two females and two males. Each member of the team was given a small task to do that would contribute to completing the task. The first meeting where they reported, Female A had not done her work. She claimed to have been sick. The second meeting, Female A still did nothing and claimed the books were out of the library. Other team members were openly getting irritated by this type of irresponsibility. The third meeting came, a different story from Female A who still had nothing to contribute. This time the deadline was close and the group had to put the project together. Female B pointed to female A that what she was doing was wrong as it stunted progress. Female A took what Female B said with anger. Verbal fighting started with Female A throwing some insults to Female B which ended with the male students reporting the incident to the facilitator as they could not continue working with Female A.

After presenting the case, the facilitator let learners analyze what has happened. She prepared some questions to guide learners' reactions, for example,

- How best do you think Female A should have handled the complaint from Female B?
- Do you think it was wise for the group to let Female A make three excuses in a row for not having done her part of the assignment?
- What evidence do you have to believe that indeed Female A is responsible but it was just circumstances beyond her control that pushed her to be considered irresponsible?
- What could be done to avoid a situation like this one?
- What will make the team go back together, if there is need?

Many questions were asked to help learners reflect on the situation and to learn from it.

Analyzing of the Case

The facilitator gave this project in good faith, to develop learners' teamwork skills. Something went wrong with the way the activity was handled. Learners gave some observations and a number of comments. Then, the facilitator reflected on them to help her class to compile principles of teamwork. These included the following

- ✓ Going into a team comes along with commitment and responsibility, if you are not prepared for this, leave the team intact not shattered.
- ✓ Report 'free-riders' as soon as you spot them, you leave them ride on you, they will continue to ride on others.
- ✓ Learning is a responsibility. Don't expect to be rewarded for doing nothing, that is, irresponsibility gets you nowhere.
- ✓ Do what other team members do. Don't try to be different when you are not.
- ✓ Take teamwork serious, it's a free and spontaneous way of building relationship and to learn together as colleagues.

Case 22 does not illustrate that most group work projects fail. On the contrary, many work perfectly well.

Skills promoted through group work

Group is useful in a number of ways.

- It is a way of developing cooperation skills—it helps group members to see the need to cooperate, failing which the project does not succeed. The interaction and synergy produced is what leads to true learning.

- It is good in developing learners' thinking skills—not everything that they read will go into the project. It takes them to think about the right information, time, resources and all that is needed to make the project a success.
- It instills in learners the spirit of responsibility—those who do not do their tasks demonstrate their irresponsibility. I do not believe it is good for any person to go around displaying this kind of behavior. Learners should learn to be responsible especially that there are consequences for being irresponsible.
- It prompts learners to respect others. Respect here means each learner in a team has to be considerate of the feelings of others. You need to know that being responsible will make other team members proud of you and respect you in return. Being irresponsible and intolerant takes you nowhere as a learner in a learning community environment. Working with others in a peaceful manner is a good sign of respect. All should respect and shall be respected.
- Group work can foster collaboration skills. Learners in a group learn to work together. The collaboration is greatly enhanced when learners are asked to share their information.
- There is no doubt that group work is good at developing learners' reasoning skills. To produce a piece that everyone in the team calls mine means each member has contributed. Team members have argued; reasoned their contribution together and decided to select what best makes a piece that each and all can identify with.

Group does not only engage learners actively, it also gives them the opportunity to acquire the skills of living together, sharing and everything else about what it means to be a group member. Negative behaviors can be turned into positive ones just by realizing that 'I do not fit with others'. It is, therefore, upon learners to be actively engaged in activities that give them skills for helping them to be 'part of' not 'apart from' others.

The other issue that Case 22 brings out is the importance of communicating well with others. Teamwork is impossible when poor interpersonal skills are encountered. The importance of a healthy communication is expressed by Shotter (1993) saying, "our daily lives are not written text or in contemplative reflection but in oral encounters and reciprocal speech (p.322). Communication can break or make a strong team. We have seen what happened in Case 22. As soon as learners forgot to respect each other and to follow a basic principle of listening to each other, the team broke up. Learners denied themselves knowledge that could have been gained by sharing and learning together. Let us be reminded that teamwork is fragile. This fragility is expressed by Galbraith (1990) who likens the working relationship to a "gossamer thread that weaves itself through various characteristics of each person present in the learning experience, that, the thread is fragile and when poor interpersonal skills are exercised, it snaps apart" (p. 7). Thus, group work survives on good communication skills.

Tips for using group work

- Always select a topic for the group to do.
- Determine what has to be achieved and how the group will make this possible.
- The goal for doing group work needs to be clearly stated and understood by learners prior to going in groups and starting their projects.
- The activity that learners are to do also needs to be clearly explained. Don't make it too cumbersome or ambiguous to

the extent that it forces learners to spend more time trying to understand what the facilitator wants.

- In giving group work, dyads or more than two learners may work together. The number should be determined by the tasks that have to be performed in the group and the products that accompany such a task.
- A project like Case 22 does not have to be done in one lesson. It can extend to other lessons with tasks continuing from the previous ones.

Group work is a respected strategy in adult education and other fields of social sciences. There is, therefore, need for the facilitator to ensure a richer experience for learners. Learners too have a role to play in the success of this strategy. If the experience is not well planned, anything worse, like what happened in the Case 22 can happen.

Partnership/networking skills

Partnership as a pedagogical strategy means learners establish a learning relationship with people outside their schools like organizations in the community. Organizations found in some communities include non-governmental organizations (NGOs), community-based organizations (CBOs) and business organizations. Associations like Famers', village and district extension teams are also part of the communities. Learners may network with these organizations in a number of ways, for example, voluntarism and formal attachments. Learners may volunteer to go to the libraries to read a story or books to the young ones who visit libraries. Government agencies may also make available materials on government services at their workplaces for learners to access them.

The discussion on using partnership as a learning strategy is similar to what has already been said about the internship or voluntarism. Thus, instead of making a lengthy presentation on partnerships, I provide just the tips for using them and refer readers to discussions on these related topics, voluntarism and placement or internship. The following are, therefore, some practical tips for using partnership as a learning strategy.

 ## Some practical tips for using partnership

- Think of engaging learners in partnership with other organizations only when you are convinced that this strategy will contribute essential information leading to the achievement of your learning objectives.
- Forming partnership is a process that must be undertaken when there are resources for it, for example, when it can be fitted in the class timetables.
- The content and context provided by the host institution/ organization should be conducive for learning. Certainly, partnership as a learning strategy is not a matter of just finding out a willing partner, but it is more about the learning that accrues from this type of learning environment.
- Learners who are to engage in partnership for learning should know what it is they are expected to do as partners. It is good to engage them when you are convinced they have skills and behaviors to sustain or make the partnership work well.
- Finding partners begins by making inquiry or profiles of organizations in the community and the type of work they do. This helps in finding a field relevant to the area of learners' interest.

An activity

This activity will help you reflect on the skills that have been explored in this chapter. The activity requires you to indicate what you consider to be the important skills and 'not so important' ones for your community.

Cooperation and collaboration	Highly needed	Occasionally needed	Not needed	Comments
Respect				
Responsibility				
Communication				
Appreciative				
Accommodation				
Thinking				
Considerate				
Tolerance				

- What aspects of your culture indicate that cooperation/ collaboration skills are part of your living together as a community?
- Think of activities or projects that can help build partnership between your institution and other organizations in the community.
- What other strategies do you know of that facilitators can use to build these important skills of cooperation and collaboration?

CHAPTER 9
HONING SOCIAL RESPONSIBILITY SKILLS

Being responsible means doing the right thing and taking charge. Sometimes it means admitting your mistakes; it means taking care of yourself and sometimes it means taking care of others (Aloian & Miller, 2010).

Introduction

One of the mistakes that we facilitators make is to assume that all learners are responsible for their learning. Experiences for most of us have taught us that some will simply not do their assignments perhaps until the last day when they come to the facilitator with all sorts of excuses. Some skip classes without any good reasons but just because they do not feel like going to classes. Others are known to go to class and not bother to take some notes and when examinations approach, they borrow notebooks to photocopy and study from notes written by others. What really is responsible about these acts? Of course, there are some who are responsible but this does not preclude us facilitators from promoting responsibility skills.

Responsibility is defined as ability to act without guidance or supervision. Learners have an obligation to ensure that they succeed in their learning; this is a sign of responsibility. As Kurtus (2001) says, a responsible person can be trusted or depended upon to do things on his or her own.

Attributes for being responsible

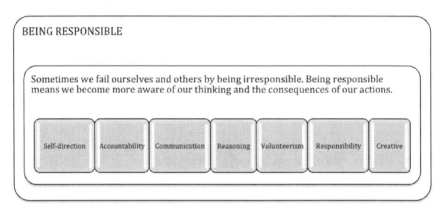

Developing skills for being responsible

A number of strategies can be used to teach learners skills for being responsible. In this chapter, voluntarism and mentoring are explored.

Voluntarism as a learning strategy

The concept as used here means that a learner takes initiatives to willingly participate in an activity or project. Even if the activity does not involve some compensation or reward, the learner is attracted because of the learning or knowledge she or he will emerge with. Just giving up a little bit of your free time to go to the library and reading books to young children who are not yet fluent in reading is an act of voluntarism. You may even help researchers to administer survey questionnaires. All these activities embody an important principle of freely contributing to help others and this is what voluntarism is all about.

To act on your decision to volunteer not because you expect compensation is done on rare occasions and yet it is very important. It promotes the use of other important skills such as being self-directed, independent, initiative, reasoning and accountable. It really needs to be encouraged. This can be done in a variety of ways. An example is given below.

Case 23: Voluntary learning encouraged

> Professor Mpho knows that during the winter holidays some learners always complain of being home doing nothing. He encourages his learners to engage in volunteer work during this time. He does this by posing a question, 'if I plan to use your time for this coming winter holidays, that is, you don't go home but engage in voluntary project of moving about the community identifying children who are poor and can do with a little soup every day, then, we go around requesting for soup contribution. Will you be willing to join me?' He pauses for learners to reflect on what he just said.

The following are some of the responses to Professor Mpho's suggestion.

> Learner A: For that period, I would like to find a temporary work with the Banks. I want to make money

for my next semester, unless of course your voluntary work will pay me.

Learner B: I think that when you volunteer, you do not expect to be paid. Am I right?

Learner C: Where have you seen this happening? Just going around and helping other people live well when you yourself do not have life? This is new to me. I don't think I can work for nothing.

Learner D: I don't mind being part of this project. We all have received help of some kind from other people. I don't see anything wrong with us helping others.

Learner E: Me too, will join the team. But just one question-Are you going to give us grades for this work? How do we actually start it? It sounds interesting but difficult to imagine how to go about it.

Professor senses that he needs some more clarifications or even some examples or illustrations of how voluntarism works. He has helped some learners who have initiated their volunteer projects by writing supporting letters. Professor asks if some learners who have done it before could share their experiences.

This is a story of one of the learners Professor has assisted in finding a host where she volunteered.

Yes, Professor helped me get an organization that I spent five weeks with, helping in planning and running of the training workshops. I was given a mentor who worked with me all the time. Luckily, this was an area that I have a lot of experience with. My advice to you is to always consider what you want to volunteer on based on the experiences you have. Your experiences help build your confidence of doing what you say you want to do. I also chose to do my work with MIED Consultants because they are known country-wide for running good programs so I was convinced I would learn a lot from them. I specifically targeted training programs because upon completion I am going to work as a trainer. I wanted to get the nitty-gritty's of being a responsible trainer. Of course, I shouldn't forget to tell you that I did the training for free (voluntary) except getting what other participants were getting like training materials, snacks and lunch. I can't regret any single moment of being with MIED, because, guess what? This is where I am going to work when I complete my degree. I have a letter from the company recruiting me. The letter says, 'MIED has seen what they are looking for in a trainer—hard work, initiative, people's skills, you name it'.

The Professor summarizes what this learner has said, by saying, 'so far two things have been made clear, (i) that voluntarism can be done and it gives rich learning experiences. The learner who shared with you demonstrated this 'doability'; (ii) You stand to reap a lot from your volunteer work. See, the learner who just shared got a job as a result of marketing herself through volunteer work.

Professor continues to sell his idea of volunteering during the summer holidays. He says, 'I have indicated my interest to work with you in doing a volunteer work. Are you interested? Although I have suggested what we can volunteer with, we can think of alternatives if you do not want this one. So, will you consider my request? If you will, please come to my office.'

Professor also reminded the class that, from the experiences of their colleague, they should realize that a person does not just go into voluntary work without important guideposts. For example,

- Choose something that appeals to your interest and perhaps what you have experiences on.
- Volunteer where you believe you have some expertise and especially when your confidence tells you that you will make it.
- Think about the benefits to get from voluntary work, for example, how it will contribute to your day-to-day work, schooling or what you would like to do in the future.
- Ensure that there is enough time to complete the voluntary work you propose.
- I am also sure that you would like to work with organizations or people that you know will not disappoint you, just as much as you wouldn't disappoint them.
- Be clear of what you want to accomplish from voluntary work. This will help you to focus your attention on something worthwhile.

These are some guidelines that can make your voluntary work memorable and fruitful.

Skills promoted through voluntary work

- Self-direction and initiation—You don't need to wait to be invited to participate in a project or activity, but take action and initiate your own learning experience. Remember to take this step when you believe you have what it takes to be involved, like necessary skills, time for the work, interest and motivation to sustain your stay in the project until it completes or until that time when the project can do without your contribution. Every instance of voluntarism is a rich experience for developing tangible skills useful for lives outside the four walls of the classrooms.

- Decision-making—To volunteer means thinking about different alternatives and opting for the one that will give rich and thick experiences. To choose from alternatives is to make decision, thus voluntarism aids decision-making skills.

- Critical thinking skill—Being a critical thinker is part of what will make you a good volunteer. It is possible that you may engage in a voluntary work only to find out as you start that what you expected is not exactly what is coming out of the activity. Don't quit immediately. A responsible learner will try to ask as many questions as possible to understand whether indeed there are some differences and the possible causes. In other words, open your mind to a number of possibilities. There may be good reasons why things are not as you expected them or have been promised. Also, ensure that you do not compromise your emotions and skills too much. If you feel the activity has turned to be something else than what you expected, communicate this in a logical and diplomatic manner. You wouldn't want to anger anyone who can be your potential source of learning and employment in the future.

- Goal setting and accountability—I take that we all get engaged in a task, activity or project with a hope of accomplishing and getting something from it. A sense of accomplishment makes one to own and identify with what she or he has done. This builds accountability too.

Finally, we may summarize our discussion on voluntarism by borrowing some important quotation from the Centre for Community Enterprise (2000) that states that

> Young people in search of work options can use volunteering to boost their resume with good work experiences. Others can make local connections in the field of their choice that may lead to actual work, mentoring, support, etc. In some cases, volunteering provides much needed practical experiences. In every case, voluntarism demonstrates to potential employers that a person is committed and proactive (p. 54).

The benefits derived from doing volunteer work are many as the quotation above indicates. Facilitators should, therefore, encourage learners to engage in this activity.

Mentoring

A mentor is explained as "someone with years of experience and knowledge that can be tapped to benefit others junior to them who aspire to go through similar experiences or professional experiences" (Centre for Community Enterprise, 2000:64). Mentoring, then, when used as a learning strategy means that a learner chooses someone (in-person or as portrayed in the literature) who can help clarify or provide pertinent information about a specific area of study. This is someone that learners can ask questions when they do not understand.

In my classes, I normally employ what I call 'surrogate mentors' because the books that we use as sources of subject matter are written by people outside the country. This makes physical interaction difficult. Instead of being hopeless because my learners cannot get someone close by to learn from, I use what I prefer to call surrogate mentors, not pseudo or fake. They are not fake but real because we learn from the books that they have written. The ideas are real and theirs. The only thing we miss is the direct or physical interaction with them. Thus, we interact with their ideas in the literature.

Surrogate mentors

Surrogate mentoring is an effective strategy when you want to encourage learners to be responsible for their learning. Learners are encouraged to interact with the literature. The interaction becomes real as one questions, interacts and communicates with these surrogate mentors. Learners carefully follow the line of thinking of the mentor, question the way the mentors think and plans what she or he wants to gain from these mentors' experiences and ideas as presented in their writings. The learners' most important role is to ask the right questions as guided by the course outline. Once an area of investigation has been selected, the mentor influences the learner's assignments and becomes a framework for thinking.

Below I explained how I use 'surrogate' mentors in my class but where learners can get someone they can interact directly with, they are encouraged. From a strategic point of view, learners are not encouraged to try to communicate with a mentor who is far from them. Issues of resources and duration of the course can make this impossible.

Case 24: A case of mentoring

Usually when I introduce the use of surrogate mentors in my class for the first, learners seem confused about this strategy. The type of questions asked indicate this confusion or fear that they may not get the right person to study. However, further explanation gets the learners interested. For example, I give detailed explanation of how we will use it in class. Examples, I explain that (i) learners will select a topic from the course outline (ii) then make an annotated bibliography of authors who write on the topic selected (iii) This is followed by reading not less than five articles by different authors on the selected topic (iv) learners then write questions that they would like see answered about the topic they have selected (v) What then follows is selecting the one author that a learner believes is likely to give him or her the best answers to the questions (vi) then each prepares a presentation for class based on critical questions asked and best lessons from the mentor.

The idea for giving this type of assignment with a number of sub-topics is to help the learners familiarize themselves with the literature before choosing the right mentor. Learners are responsible for ensuring that they read widely enough to make wise choices. The facilitator meets regularly with learners to ensure that they, at least, select contents aligned to the course outline and the objectives of the course. All items (steps) indicated in the case above are assignments that the facilitator grades, for example, (i) topic of discussion (ii) annotated bibliography on this topic (iii) selection of a single author as a point of reference. Learners are also advised to prepare a list of other authors who will complement and those with different perspectives. This is a way of enriching their presentation, (iv) the presentation (usually a power-point is encouraged). This presentation comprises the main assignment. The facilitator usually checks it before being presented in class.

As you may realize, this strategy is effective with small classes of 10-15 learners. I usually use it with my graduate learners. Really, if there is time, it can be employed even with undergraduate learners.

Skills that learners develop from using mentoring as a learning strategy

A number of skills can be developed or promoted through the use of mentoring. These include the following;

- Studying a mentor is a process that develops one's analytic, evaluative and critical thinking skills. The learners is bound to question, to analyze, evaluate and make conclusions about the information provided by the mentor, especially as some mentors come in 'book/printed material' form.
- Learners develop skills for interacting with books, in a case of surrogate mentors. Eventually, the interaction becomes real as one questions, interacts and communicates with them.
- Learners learn to be responsible for making a follow up on questions that he or she wants to ask the mentor. For some, especially those who get real and not surrogate mentors, they may contact them if they want some clarifications about what the mentor has said or at times when they want the next line of thinking on the same topic. Some learners are even influenced to use the mentor's ideas as a basis for their research or career advancement. The experience for many is very informative and can shape behavior and attitude towards learning.

Tips for using mentoring as a learning strategy

The course outline usually comes with clear guidelines of how to choose a surrogate mentor or real one where possible. As I have already indicated, in my situation, a real mentor is impossible for now as we use books written by outsiders. The expectation for a mentee is explained and come together with responsibilities such as

- How to establish an interest in a mentor—making an annotated bibliography of a chosen topic from the course outline.
- Following up on a professional life of a mentor.
- Researching a specific topic related to the mentor's area of interest.
- Being a 'class expert' in the area you have chosen—present a well prepared presentation of the topic you have selected, write a short report of your learning experiences with this mentor indicating knowledge and skills gained.
- Write a short reflective journal of how 'becoming an expert' in the area has benefited you and colleagues. Studying this mentor is always part of an effective learning process.
- Mentees who are serious to learn from their mentors can keep on learning beyond the class. If they envy the skills their mentors have, they will do whatever it takes them as learners to develop some of these skills.

An activity

A number of skills have been discussed in this chapter. Remind yourself of them by doing the following activity.

Responsibility Skills	Highly needed	Occasionally needed	Not needed	Comments
Self-direction				
Initiative				
Analytic				
Thinking				
Decision-making				
Communication				
Appreciative				
Voluntarism				
Exploration				

- Ask learners to share experiences in which being irresponsible has simply messed up what could have been a good project.
- What steps should be taken to ensure that other learners do not 'ride' on others during group work (use others to do their assignments)
- What other strategies have you used to develop learners' responsible skills?

PART 3

REFLECTIONS AND PLOUGHBACKS

Part 3 summarizes the main lessons learned in this book. It reflects on the goals of learning, the philosophy of engaged learners and principles supporting the discussions on functional learning. Strategies for engaging learners in developing community skills are also summarized. A chapter is brought in presenting a model for 'engaging learners'. Still, the author claims that what is contained in this book does not provide absolute answers to the questions that educators ask themselves as they prepare and engage in learning for the development of community skills. The author implores educators or facilitators to do more research to complement and supplement the examples presented in this book. However, the information given is good enough to arouse interest in and guide those with the desire to develop important community skills.

CHAPTER 10
EXPERIENCES AND LESSONS

All of us with hands clasped, eyes to the future, hope stamped
on our faces can help reform learning systems that do not
address the needs of our local communities (Searle, 1981).

Introduction

This book has three parts. Each part makes certain claims about
learning and its purposes within a philosophy of 'engaged learners'.
The first part illustrates the major philosophies behind the idea
of effective or functional learning as presented in this book. Part
two starts to interrogate characteristics of learning systems with
capabilities to imbue learners with functional community skills.
Rather, a certain type of learners, 'the engaged learners' are said to
be a necessary pre-requisite for making the development of functional
skills possible. Even with the presence of these learners, the context
of learning is incomplete if learners themselves (their characteristics,
learning aspirations and cultures) and contents of learning have not
been considered.

Part three of this book explores the key lessons of this book—
community functional skills. Efforts to promote functional skills
are based on an understanding that all of us deserve to live better

as a result of our education or learning. Skills here are considered as capabilities, talents and abilities that people can use to improve their lives together with those of community members. The term community is used broadly here to mean lives outside the classroom environments. A number of skills emerge from chapters in this section. In trying not to present abstract accounts of these skills, some illustrations and case studies have been provided. All these are meant to emphasize that our engagement should not only be at a theoretical level but should include practice.

The strategies have been chosen because of what they can offer. This means that the focus is not on strategies per se but on the principles guiding them. The importance of considering principles behind using a strategy is explained by Jackson (2009), who claims that there are millions of strategies, but principles are few. He believes that facilitators who understand the principles can successfully select their preferred strategies. Clearly, using the right strategy is dependent on the facilitator's knowledge and ingenuity. The facilitator has to be clear of why a particular strategy is the best for developing certain skills. It is, therefore, advisable to find out what is unique about a particular strategy to make it qualify for promoting the skills you want to promote. In short, the strategies used have to be chosen carefully.

The final part reflects and summarizes the major lessons of the book. It persuades facilitators to put learners in the centre of learning. This implies that for learners to be responsible for their learning and be motivated to learn, they should hear about worlds they live in and be made to understand and prepared for the practical realities in these worlds. Whilst offering suggestions of how facilitators can develop some skills, clearly, the onus of what to take or leave out is on the readers of this book as guided by their beliefs about learning and its functions. Finally, a model of engaging learners is presented as part of the argument for driving home the philosophy of 'engaged learners' as promoted in this book.

Learning and its purposes

The book starts by setting a tone for the need for community functional skills. The first chapters illustrate that the major reason for us wanting to engage in some kind of learning and especially formal learning is because we want to make a difference in our lives. We live in families, small communities, and spend most of our times in workplaces, churches and other social gatherings. We want to be functional in these settings. Thus, all of us need skills for functioning in our communities.

Functional skills are defined here as capabilities, talents and abilities that people can use to live productively with others in different settings such as the home, community and nation. Others call them life skills or survival skills. The way we live our lives after schooling is a message about our learning. Some would have learned to think, to be responsible, to be hard-working, to be adaptive, to respect, to cooperate with others, to be innovative, creative, etc. while for others, it may be a different case. We all need to emerge from the learning experiences with methodical capabilities, capacities and energies to improve our lives.

Some educators like Knowles (1973) believe that one of the pre-requisites for effective learning is for learners to be sure of why they want to learn. This is goal setting on the part of the learners. Goal setting usually helps learners to determine whether they are getting what they expect from the learning situation or not. Some of the goals are not original ideas of learners themselves but have been influenced by the significant others. For example, learners are likely to be influenced by those that they respect, trust and believe in and want to please. Like Corson (1998) advises, "there is very little that can be done for individual's identity that does not begin with the group" (p.15). Case 25 may serve as an example of this type of living with and learning from others.

Case 25: Learning through others

One 19 year-old boy of my friend once told his parent, "My mind goes back to the message my grandfather gave me in our grass roofed roundavel—'if school was only to give you some hands and brain to be a true man, you will make me proud'. The boy laments, 'My hands and brain are still empty only spiky thoughts; teachers are spiky, books are spiky, schoolmates too are spiky; and now life too is becoming spiky. I haven't yet discovered how my brain and hands will make me a true man but the teachers teach me daily. What am I missing?"

Analysis of the case

The scenario above prompts us to ask important questions such as 'Do learners more often question the relevance of their learning? Yes, all the time. One thing clear from Case 25 is that learners have specific goals for engaging in learning activities, whether personally defined or shaped by the significant others.

Many of us may have come across situations where we ask ourselves questions about what school is doing for us. These questions come when we feel that what we learn is meaningless. Questions such as 'why I am learning?' How will this be helpful in my life? How is what

I learn going to help others?' Many questions can be asked and if answers to these are not clear, learners may get discouraged like the boy in Case 25 above.

Some critics of modern education caution us that at times modern schools never permit some people to enter them; they exit only like a vanishing wish (Searle, 1981). This is so when learning has no connection with real life challenges. Many have gone to school with hopes, for example, of getting formal employment or buying a car and only to realize after completion that all this is impossible. As Searle says, their dreams have vanished. Advocating for the development of functional skills is a way to counteract situations of meaningless, irrelevance and impractical encounters that at times is a result of learning that is divorced from learners' cultures. The goal of learning as presented in the book is learning for community's ways of life, with community described broadly to encompass schools and all settings outside them.

The concept of 'engaged learners'

The concept of engaged learners have been defined. We are made to understand that

(i)   Learners are engaged all the time through interacting with their learning environments (colleagues, teachers, learning resources). When learners get engaged, they are not forced to participate. They do so because they are aware of the benefits of their engagement.

(ii) Learners enjoy to test and co-create knowledge with others outside their classrooms. They have a passion for applying what they hear and say in classrooms to social worlds, like the family, community, workplaces and other settings. This for them is a way to strengthen their senses of social responsibility. They understand that schools are like gas or petrol stations; they go there temporarily to get fuel (skills) that will drive them to success and contentment in other worlds.

(iii) When facilitators make efforts to cultivate skills such as thinking, being responsible, cooperation, collaboration, respect and others, learners are not astonished but motivated to participate because they see how they resemble their natural abilities to respond to the challenges of living.

(iv) Learners have a passion for collective learning activities. They talk with each other, discuss, share information and resolve learning issues together; for they are aware that in real worlds of families, work and community, you get rewarded for being part of and not apart from others.

(v) Enjoyment in learning comes partly as a result of learners having defined or knowing their learning goals. They know that alone, they may not make wise decisions; thus, facilitators are respected as experts, guides, mentors and models.

(vi) Learners understand that learning in classrooms gives an idea but does not take them close to or direct to reality of applying what they have learned. They want to test their practical skills (e.g. innovation, decision-making, cooperation) in other worlds. This helps them to keep on learning.

Active engagement means that facilitators help learners to discuss, act out and go out of classrooms to apply what they have learned.

Strategies for strengthening engagement

Strategies that have been discussed as good in strengthening learners' engagement include the following;

- Home visits
- Work site learning
- Dramatization and other plays
- Interactive friendship
- Voluntarism
- Internship/Placement
- Field trip
- Story-telling
- Group work
- Games
- Lecture presentation
- Analogies and metaphors
- Mentor
- Guest lecturers
- In-basket
- What-If/'What-Iffing'

Community functional skills

These are mostly 'can't do without' skills in many communities. They include the thinking, collaboration, cooperation, being responsible and practice skills. While facilitators have the highest responsibility to ensure that these skills are developed, learners too have a pedagogical obligation to contribute to their learning. Brief discussions of these skills follow.

Thinking as a key survival skill

Thinking skills are needed in all settings. To function in our homes, workplaces, communities and even international, one must think. Thus, a good reason for giving a greater thought to the teaching of thinking skills is that thinking is necessary for effective citizenship (Davis, 1993:174).

Thinking has been broadly described as 'everything that the conscious mind does' (Fernyhough, 2010). We use the conscious mind all the times, for example, when we solve problems, when we analyze issues and when we act. This, therefore, makes thinking a key survival skill for all of us (Molesworth, 2011). In this book, therefore, a chapter was devoted to the teaching of thinking skills not as a set of isolated skills but in the context of other valuable functional community skills.

Thinking can present itself in variety of forms as illustrated in the table that follows.

Skill	Understanding/Description
THINKING	Thinking allows people to make sense of the world in different ways, and to represent or interpret it in ways that are significant to them, or which accord with their needs, attachment, objectives, plans, commitments, ends and desires (http://en.wikipedia.org/wiki/Thought)
	Its typology
Creative	A way of looking at a situation from a different perspective and bringing in new perspectives or thoughts in a manner that defines value and practical intends.
Reflective	A means of reassessing a situation or self, leading to the possibilities of seeing a situation from different perspectives or coming up with different responses to it.

Critical	Being able to ask appropriate questions, gather relevant information, efficiently and creatively sort through this information, reason logically from this information, and come to reliable and trustworthy conclusions about the world that enable one to live and act successfully in it (Jensen, 2008).
Adaptive	Ability to fathom context-differences and make adjustments accordingly, especially when confronted by new and unanticipated circumstances.
Dialogical	Thinking that involves a dialogue or extended exchange between different points of view or frames of reference. Students learn best in dialogical situations, in circumstances in which they continually express their views to others and try to fit other's views into their own (http://www.criticalthinking.org/articles/ glossary.cfm).
Analytic	To examine in detail so as to determine the nature of, to look more deeply into an issue or situation. All learning presupposes some analysis of what we are learning for example, ideas, claims, experiences, interpretations, judgments, and theories and those we hear and read (http://www.criticalthinking.org/articles/ glossary.cfm).

| Reasoning | The drawing of conclusions or inferences from observations, facts, or hypotheses. A critical thinker tries to develop the capacity to transform thought into reasoning, or rather, the ability to make his or her inferences explicit, along with the assumptions or premises upon which those inferences are based. Reasoning is a form of explicit inferring, usually involving multiple steps (http://www.criticalthinking.org/articles/glossary.cfm). |

Relational and Emotional Skills

Emotional and relational skills are worthy all times. As Jensen (2008) says, "the influence of emotions in our behavior is immense because they give us a life report at all times" (p. 82). This helps us makes a case to be always concerned about undisciplined emotions because they can harm our rational thinking (Damaisio, 1994 cited in Jensen, 2008).

Obviously, many of us, perhaps all of us, value strong or healthy bonds with others. We sustain these types of bond through disciplined emotions. Similarly, healthy communities exist because of the good relationships among community members. Actually, "a real community exists only when its members interact in a meaningful way that deepens their understanding of each other and leads to learning" (Oblinger, 2006). Our learning institutions can act to inculcate the desire to relate well, live in a just and caring environments. This gives hope that upon their graduation, learners will have no problems connecting with others in other settings.

Here are some shades of these relational and emotional skills.

Skills	Understanding/Description
EMOTIONAL SKILLS	It is natural to respond to everyday situations emotionally. It is common to feel angry, sad, happy or frightened at different times. Emotional skills are a set of abilities that let you form good relationships with others in everyday life and at work. They determine an individual's response to any situation. People with good emotional skills are more likely to respond to situations appropriately and in a socially accepted manner. Emotional skills need to be well developed because we rely on social interaction in everything that we do (yssn.ca/images/clientupload/fS13.pdf). **Defining Characteristics**
Caring	It is being kind, showing that you care; expressing gratitude, forgiving others and helping people in need (Major, 2008). Care involves more than feelings or attitude of warmth towards a person or an experience. It is being mindful of the context in which the need for care arises and mindful of the need to offer support which mobilizes another person's coping strategies to circumvent the Development of codependency (Arnold, 2010).

Trustworthiness	To be honest, not to deceive, cheat or steal (Major, 2008).
Respect	To treat others as you would want to be treated and to tolerate differences (Major, 2008).
Kindness	We are kind to others not because they will appreciate us and say 'thank you' but because it is a nurturing act and the right thing to do. Acts of kindness offer hope to troubled students who feel hopeless. They affirm and strengthen the need for having a supportive relationship during stressful times (Long, 2007).
Empathy	The ability to respond positively to personal emotions and to understand and respond to the feelings of others in compassionate ways (Naested, Potvin & Waldron, 2003).
Courteous	Showing respect, politeness and being affable to other people.
Fairness	Not taking advantage of others. Not blaming others without considering your actions (Major, 2008).
Emotional intelligence	The ability to understand emotions, reflectively regulate them intelligently, like dealing with anger or disappointment in a peaceful manner (Mayer & Salovey, 1997).

Cooperation and collaboration skills

Cooperation and collaboration skills are associated with how we relate and live together with others. As Herman (1999) laments, many families, communities and the world at large seem to have lost a sense of cooperation and collaboration. For example, at the individual level, failure to communicate or be close to each other has driven some people to commit suicide; on the family level, the presence of domestic abuse may signal lack of cooperation and working together; at the national and international arenas, ills such as strikes, fighting and unending conflicts are signs that cooperation or healthy relationships are hard to find. These problems indicate that something has to be done to attend to these important virtues of our social living. Thus, the idea of teaching cooperation and collaboration skills should be attractive.

A basic understanding is that where people work cooperatively or collaboratively, no one is a dependent. They work together because they have unique strengths. Each team member has some short shortcomings that are compensated by the strengths of others. Learners should be helped to experience these dynamics of cooperatively and collaboratively working with other people.

The table below presents cooperation/collaboration and its related attributes.

Skill	Understanding/Description
COOPERATION/ COLLABORATION	The relationship of collaborators is mutual not dependent, permitting them to contribute according to personal and team strengths and to respect responsibility, rules and authority.

	Its critical defining characteristics
Accommodative	Being open to and considerate of other people's point of view and feelings.
Teamwork	Connecting together with ideas, perspectives, actions, respecting and appreciating the team's connection and goals.
Critical thinking	Being able to challenge perspectives brought forth by self and others in a manner that brings out new or refined perspectives when responding to a specified situation and intended goals.
Communication	Communication generates social consciousness and creates an ability to work on collective goals as people discuss and share their individual's and group's desires, needs and prospective actions (Jenlink, 2009).
Respect	Be considerate of the feelings of others. Use good manners, not bad language (Major, 2008).
Responsibility	Being answerable to a number of issues, such as decisions, actions, thinking and how these impact the situation in which they are exercised.
Emotional intelligence	The capacity to recognize own feelings and those of others, for motivating ourselves, for managing own emotions and relationships. Some aspects of this type of intelligence include emotional awareness, accurate self-assessment, self-confidence, self-control, trustworthiness, adaptability, initiative, optimism, understanding others, conflict management and so on (Goleman, 1998).

Skills for being responsible

Another area of skill development is 'being responsible'. Being responsible means that people are answerable to a number of issues, such as decisions, actions, thinking and how these impact the situation in which they are exercised. Running away from what you are supposed to do and its consequences is a simple way of throwing out your responsibility and opting to be named irresponsible.

In the classroom, Jackson (2009) advises that we should not assume that all learners are responsible and ask them to take responsibility without first laying the groundwork for them to do so. It is critical that overt strategies be planned for promoting skills for being responsible. We are quite aware of situations in which lack of these skills have led to behaviors such as negligence of duty, avoidance of work or just simply abandoning what you are supposed to do. Some disturbances, disappointments or conflict cannot be avoided where a person chooses to be irresponsible.

Below are some more insights into the skills for being responsible.

Skill	Understanding/Description
BEING RESPONSIBLE	Is doing what you are supposed to do, persevering and always doing your best. It's about being self-disciplined, thinking and considering the consequences before you act (Major, 2008).
Its critical defining characteristics	
Self-direction	It is about taking initiative, responsibility and being accountable for your actions.
Initiative	Denotes personal ability to look at issues from different perspectives in order to come up with new ideas or course of actions.

Creative	It overlaps with but it is not the same thing as originality. Originality requires novelty, uniqueness, unconventionality or at least unusualness. Creativity certainly requires originality but also something else as well—a kind of effectiveness or fit (Runco, 2010).
Communication	It's a process of interactional experiences involving exchange of ideas or thoughts, understanding what is being communicated and responding appropriately as one gains more respect and understanding of the what is communicated and understands the means of communication, like verbal, written and others.
Accountability	Accountability is an idea that says you are answerable for your action and inactions. If questions come up or something goes wrong, it's you who must absorb scrutiny. The willingness to be accountable for what you do and what you fail or refuse to do is a crucial sign of your character (Schiling, 2009).
Trust	Implies that your trust is based on a predictable pattern of behavior, although sometimes on hope and believing in or relying on someone or something.
Voluntarism	Taking initiatives to willingly participate in an activity or project, knowing or not expecting some compensation or reward.
Reasoning	Capacity to listen or understand, question, think and engage in logical argument or discussion addressing a specific point of discussion.

Action-oriented/Practice Skills

Practice fuses a number of skills—the thinking, cooperation, collaboration, being responsible and others. Moreover, these are not fused and applied in a vacuum. The application takes place in complex environments like homes, communities and workplaces. Important aspects of practical skills are shown in the table that follows.

Practical skills

Skill	Understanding/Description
Practice	Refers to the ability to translate abstraction and theories into realistic applications. Students apply, put into practice, implement, employ and render practical ideas (Baldwin, 2010).
	Its critical defining characteristics
Adaptive	Ability to fathom changes in one's environment (social context) and respond to satisfy the challenges or problem in a specific context.
Contextual	Understanding the social context of your actions or thinking.
Decision-making	It involves generating considerations and determining the options to get to the end result, and then selecting the most suitable option to achieve the desired purpose (Burden & Byrd, 2007).
Collaboration	Collaboration is working together to achieve a goal, (http://en.wikipedia.org/wiki/Collaboration)
Cooperation	Ability to relate and live together with others.

Analytic	It requires critical thinking, which in turn brings into play convergent thinking. Ideas are sorted out, and the best conclusions are reached. Students who learn analytic skills are drawn into an exploration, critiquing, judging, comparing, contrasting, evaluating and assessing (Baldwin, 2010).
Responsibility	Ability to think and act reasonably and effectively without necessarily needing guidance.
Problem solving	The process by which a situation is analyzed and solutions are formed to solve a **probortunity** (i.e. problem/opportunity) and steps are taken to remove or reduce the problem (http://www.brainstorming.co.uk/tutorials/definitions.html)

Essentials of knowledge base

A position taken in this book is that for all fields of practices, there is a fundamental knowledge base that professionals in that particular field should know. These are theories. Most of us assume that practice is indeed guided by theories or still, as may be argued, that practice helps to enrich and come up with more theories. These theories must be taught as they act as our lines of thoughts.

The skills that are promoted through teaching theories and other idea include the following;

Skill	Understanding/Description
CONCEPTUAL	Conceptually thinking is the ability to understand a problem or situation by identifying and addressing key underlying issues and constraints (conceptskills.wikispaces.com)
	Its critical defining characteristics
Compose	Ability to identify and use words that connect to describe a main concept or theory.
Analyze	Looking at, understanding and describing a pattern in something, for example, in an event or story.
Describing	Giving an account in words of someone or something, including relevant characteristics, qualities or events (Merriam Webster, The Free Dictionary).
Examination	Ability to question statements or responses made by others by observing how they logically flow or interrelate to give substance, meaning or worth.

This chapter has given an elaborate account of community skills. Other ideas that may help us to expand this notion of community functional skills are those framed around philosophies of cultural learning, lifelong learning, democratic education, pedagogies of freedom or peace, civic education or educating for citizenship. These call for contextualization of our learning systems. They prompt us to understand that learning is all about developing our abilities, capabilities and potentials to think, to relate well with others, to be responsible, to solve problems, be accountable and to cope with changes and intricacies of the practical worlds.

CHAPTER 11
THE IMPLEMENTABLE

Introduction

All of us need to ask serious questions about what we teach and how we teach. The chapters in this book do not provide absolute answers to all questions that we ask ourselves but they illustrate ways in which some of these questions can be answered. The discussions have been focused on some very important questions, like, the goals of learning, the contents of learning and critical skills that we believe are needed by everyone to live productively. These are provided as examples of a relevant or meaningful learning program as indicated below.

The goals of learning

First, suggestions have been made as to what could be the possible learning goals. These suggestions are summarized below in a table that has been adapted from Lekoko and Modise (2011). Few modifications have been made to suit the contents of this book.

Major goals of learning

Learning as a social goal	It is learning that shifts attentions from values of grades and competition to the development of community skills
Both technical and soft skills are highly valued	We learn to do, work together and respect. Learning that develops soft skills (solidarity, trust, respect, networking and shared values) is mostly valued.
The focus is on learners and learning rather than teachers and teaching	Learning recognizes learners as critical resources for learning. Thus, learners are engaged all the time with facilitators guiding and supporting them.
Lifelong learning strategies as guiding principles	Learning in a micro sense on the classroom floor is not better than learning in the macro sense of community's challenges or ways of life in which learning never ends. Learners learn to keep on learning.
Inter-active dialogue is one of critical learning strategies	Learners have a passion for discussion to broaden their perspectives of their social worlds. Learning is building interactive friendships.
Learning is essentially for day-to-day existence: You learn or starve or survive	Learners use what they learn in their real life challenges. It is learning if it can be applied to situations present outside the classroom walls.
Learning survives on learners' understanding of themselves as citizens of certain communities	Learning is imbuing learners the need to belong, with tools for self-criticism, a pride to identify with and a strong sense of belongingness to one's community

Skills development

Not all the teaching strategies presented in the table below have been used in this book. Most of the facilitators have used different strategies and are trained well to know the best strategies for developing specific skills.

Teaching method	Description
Field trip	It involves going out of classroom to other setting like homes, workplaces and communities to experience a learning environment of real application or observations of challenges and responding to them.
Discussion	A process of engaging learners in a conversation or dialogue geared towards a specified learning objective. It promotes collective work and exchange of experiences.
Observation	A process of guiding learners to examine or watch real life actions and learning from them for personal and collective gain.
Word Play/Puzzle	A game used to help learners learn concepts—learners search words, find their association and meanings and use them to describe or give some characteristics of a particular concepts or theory like andragogy. This process promotes good thinking skills.
Brainstorming	A means of generating ideas around a topic that learners later find useful in the learning that particular topic.
Guest lecturing	Inviting a professional or person with trusted sources of expertise or knowledge of a topic being discussed to shed light on some practical experiences of it.
Group work	Arranging learners in groups to learn a particular subject matter that prompts them to go beyond individual's thinking to a group's understanding of the topic through a process that makes it possible for members to acquire the skills of working and living together.

Short conversational lecture	Teacher's explanation or definition of the subject matter usually done as a background or introduction to some contents that need detailed exploration especially by the learners.
Learning friendship	Learners learn from each other, not from a teacher. They can form their own groups and interact both in and outside the classroom to collectively learn the subject matter. The arrangement is learner-guided.
Dramatisation	Social problems are acted out, following the logic of action in real life situation. They interpret these actions in relation to social value and significance/signification. As Kicheloe, Slattery and Steinberg (2000) say, "play promotes a freedom and fairness conducive to creativity. It is some highest expressions of human endeavours" (p. 179).
In-basket	A situation where learners apply their analytic skills to a given description of a social issue/problem after which they identify alternative actions pointing to new and different directions.
Partnerships	A meeting where people come together to discuss a particular problem for common or collective good. This involves proper identification of the problem, causes of the problem, and possible actions to alleviate the problem.
Critical incident process	The focus is to identify and analyze incidents that lead to change in behavior or condition. For instance, sharing how one overcomes certain social or economic hardships or attained success from adverse conditions.

Debate	Is a play or action that brings learners close to experiencing a possible life challenge or problem as they think, argue and think of possible means or addressing or solving the issue.
Home visits	Learners are sent to different homes to share and learn with families.
Voluntarism	Learners take initiatives to participate in a project or activity for the sake of acquiring knowledge and skills useful to their lives and without anticipation of compensation of any type.
Mentoring	Learners choose someone (in person or in the literature) with years of experiences and knowledge to study as guided by class course outline or specific learning objectives.
'What-If'	Giving learners a 'what-if' scenario that demands them to think about the situation as currently experienced and develop different strategies based on the guidelines as presented in the learning activity.
Analogy/metaphor	Using an object or imagination to explain an understanding of a concept.

Engaging learners

Throughout this book, facilitators have been implored to actively engage learners in what they learn. Engagement, as claimed, starts with learners understanding and making meaning out of what they learn. The book presents a teaching-learning model that treats community as equally a vital resource for learning that can be complemented by traditional resources like books and teacher-resourcefulness. The model of learning is presented below.

Model of engaging learners

Community as a Resource for Learning   Community Functional Skills

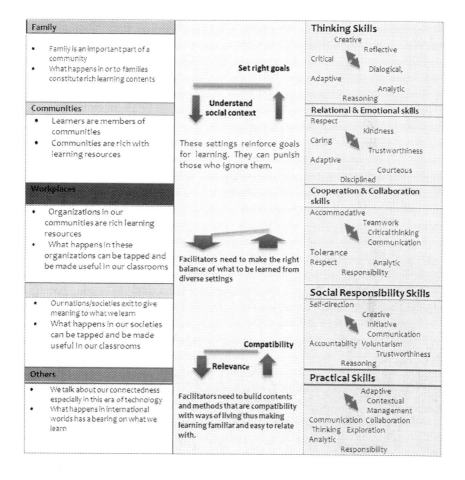

Those of us interested in developing community skills can use the graphic above to think of these skills and those that may have been overlooked. Transforming our educational activities to address these skills is something that we can tackle collaboratively or individually.

After all, ideas, commitment to learning and change starts in the hearts of individuals. I, therefore, want to end this book by stressing that regardless of your position in your organization, as long as in one way or the other you take part in facilitating the learning process, you can commit to making learning a true asset to our communities.

Thought-Provoking Questions

As we read and use this book in our educational or learning encounters, we may like to reflect on a number of questions.

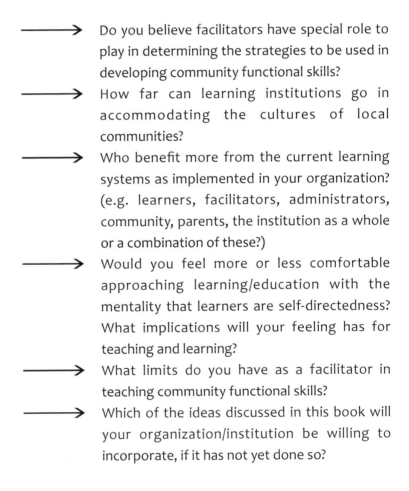

⟶ Do you believe facilitators have special role to play in determining the strategies to be used in developing community functional skills?

⟶ How far can learning institutions go in accommodating the cultures of local communities?

⟶ Who benefit more from the current learning systems as implemented in your organization? (e.g. learners, facilitators, administrators, community, parents, the institution as a whole or a combination of these?)

⟶ Would you feel more or less comfortable approaching learning/education with the mentality that learners are self-directedness? What implications will your feeling has for teaching and learning?

⟶ What limits do you have as a facilitator in teaching community functional skills?

⟶ Which of the ideas discussed in this book will your organization/institution be willing to incorporate, if it has not yet done so?

BIBLIOGRAPHY

Aloian, M. and Miller, R. (2010). *Juvenile audience.* Ontario: St. Catharines.

Anderson, D. R. (2000). Character education: Who is responsible? *Journal of Instructional Psychology,* 27 93), 139-142.

Arnold, R. (2010). Empathic intelligence in educational therapy. In M. Ficksman and J. Adellizi, (Eds.), *The clinical practice of educational therapy: A teaching model.* New York: Routledge.

Baldwin, A. (2010). Creativity: A look outside the box in classrooms. In R. Beghetto and J. KaufmN, (EDS), Nurturing creativity in the classrooms. Cambridge: University Press, pp. 73-87.

Bowers, C. (1993). *Critical essays on education, modernity, and the recovery of the ecological imperative.* New York: Teachers College Press.

Braman, S. (1996). Interpenetrated globalization: Scaling, power and public sphere. In S. Braman and A. Sreberny-Mohammadi, (Eds.), *Globalization, communication and transnational civil society.* Greenskill, NJ: Hampton Press, pp. 21-37.

Brown, p. Bovey, J. and Chen, X. (1997). Context-aware application: From laboratory to marketplace. *IEEE Personal Communication,* 4 (5); 58-64.

Burden, P. and Byrd, D. (2007). *Methods for effective teaching.* Boston: Pearson.

Chambers, R. (2003). *Whose reality counts? Putting the first last.* London: ITDG Publishing.

Charles, L. (2008). *Succeeding as an international student in the United States and Canada.* Chicago: University of Chicago press.

Cleaver, F. 2001. 'Institutions, agency and the limitations of participatory approaches to development. In B. Cooke. And U. Kothari (Eds.) *Participation: The new tyranny?* London: Zed Books, pp. 36-55.

Coeckelbergh, M. Social transformation and the right to communication: An Introduction and a proposal fro a capacity approach to ethics of ICTs. Retrieved April 17, 2011 from http://groups.itu.int/LinkClick.aspx?tabid=1229&FileTicket=05226.

Cohen, J. (1999). Learning about social and emotional learning: Current themes and future directions. In J. Cohen (Ed.), *Educating minds and hearts. Social emotional learning and the passage into adolescence.* New York: Teachers College, Columbia University, pp.184-190.

Corson, D. (1998). *Changing education for diversity.* Buckingham: Open University Press.

Council for Higher Education Accreditation (CHEA) CHEA Institute for Research and Study of Accreditation and Quality Assurance, 2003, *Statement Of Mutual Responsibilities for Student Learning Outcomes: Accreditation, Institutions, and Programs,* September 2003. Retrieved April 16 2011 from at http://www.chea.org/Research/index.asp

Council of Chief State School Officers (1991). Connecting school and employment. Retrieved April 08, 2011. *http://www.ccsso.org/About_the_Council.*

Cyrtis, M. and Shah, H. (2010). *Reorienting global communication: Indians and Chinese media beyond borders.* Urbana: University of Illinois Press.

David, C. (2005). *College knowledge: What it really takes for students to succeed and what we can do to get them ready.* San Francisco: Jossey-Bass.

Davis, J. (1993). *Better teaching more learning: Strategies for success in postsecondary settings.* American Council on Education, Series on Higher Education: ORYX Press.

Dewey, J. (1927). *The public and its problems.* New York: Henry Holt.

Dewey, J. (1916). *Democracy and education: An introduction to the philosophy of education.* New York: Macmillan.

Dewey, J. (1938). *Experience and education.* New York: Collier Books.

Dewey, J. (1939). *Freedom and culture.* New York: Putman.

Dey, A. (1998). Context-aware computing. *Spring Symposium on Intellectual Environment, Technical Report* SS-98, pp. 51-54.

Dilts, R. (1996). The new leadership paradigm. Retrieved December 15, 2010 from http://www.nlpu.com/Articles/article8.htm

Elton, L. (2011). Complexity theory: An approach to assessment that can enhance learning and transform university management. In, M. Molesworth, R. Scullion, and E. Nixon, *The marketisation of higher education and the student as a consumer.* London: Routlege, pp. 64-70.

Erickson, F. (2004). *Talk and social theory.* Cambridge: Polity Press

Fata-Hartley, C. (2011). Resting rote learning: The importance of active learning for all course objectives. *Journal of College Science Teaching, pp. 36-39.*

Fernyhough, C. (2010). What do we mean by thinking? Retrieved February 201, from http://www.psychologytoday.com/blog/the-child-in-time/201008/what-do-we-mean-thinking

Flores, M. and Day, C. (2006). Context which shape and reshape new teachers' identities: A multiperspective study. *Teaching and Teacher Education,* 22 (2); 219-232.

Franquis, R. (2010). *The origins of responsibility.* Bloomington: Indiana University Press.

Freire, P. (1998). *Pedagogy of freedom: Ethics, democracy and civic courage.* Lanham, MD: Rowman and Littlefield.

Friedman, G. (2005). Home-to-school communication. In P. Schmidst (Ed.), *Preparing educators to communicate and connect with families and communities.* Greenwich: Information Publishing, pp. 1-18.

Galbraith, M. W. (1990). *Adult learning methods. A guide for effective instruction.* Malabar: Krieger.

Gardner, H. (2007). The ethical mind: A conversation with psychologist Howard Gardner. *Harvard Business Review,* 85(3), 51-56.

Gardner, H. (1999). Foreword. In J. Cohen (Ed.), *Educating minds and hearts. Social emotional learning and the passage into adolescence.* New York: Teachers College, Columbia University, pp. ix-xii.

Garegae, K. (Forthcoming). Experiencing the functionality of mathematical indigenous ICTs on community development: A Case of Farm House Dairy Product. In R. Lekoko and L. Semali (Eds.), Cases on developing countries and ICT integration: Rural community development. Hershey: IGI.

Garner, R. (2005). Humor, analogy and metaphor. H.A.M it up in teaching. *Radical Pedagogy,* 6(2). Retrieved May 6, 2011 from http://radicalpedagogy.icaap.org/content/issue6_2/garner.html

Gajanayake, S. (1984). Education for community development. In H. Reed and Lourghran, E., *Beyond schools: Education for economic, social and personal development.* Hardley, MA: Common Wealth Company Inc., pp. 73-96.

Gboku, M. and Lekoko, R. (2007). *Developing programmes for adult learners in Africa.* South Africa. Pearson Education.

Gesterwicki, C. (2007). *Home, School and community relations.* Australia: Thomson, Delma Learning.

Ghandi, M. (1980). *All men are brothers: Autobiographical reflections.* New York: Continuum.

Gilman, R. (1984). The learning process: Helping various parts of our mind fulfill their intentions. Retrieved May 7, 2011 from http://www.context.org/ICLIB/IC06/Gilman3.htm

Glasgrow, N. (1996). *New curriculum for new times: A guide to student-centred problem-based learning.* Thousand Oaks, CA: Corwin Press.

Goleman, D. (1998). *Working with emotional intelligence.* New York: Bantam Books.

Goss, B. (1983). *Communication in everyday life.* Belmont, Calif: Wadsworth Pub. Co.

Goss, D. (2010). Workplace issues in college: Educating adults with learning disabilities. In M. Ficksman and Adellizi, J. The clinical practice of educational therapy: A teaching model. New York: Routledge, pp. 289-310.

Glynn, S. & Takahashi, T (1998). Learning from analogy-enhanced science texts. *Journal of Research in Science Teaching,* 35, 1129-1149.

Hargreaves, A. (2003). *Teaching in the knowledge society: Education in the age of insecurity.* New York: Teachers College Press.

Harris, R. (2002). Creative thinking techniques. Retrieved March 3, 2011 from virtualsalt.com/crebook2.htm.

Hayakawa, S. (1971). *How words change our lives.* Illinois: McDougal, Little and Company.

Herman A.L. (1999). *Community, Violence and Peace.* Albany: State University of New York Press.

Higginbothan, J. (1998). Conceptual competence. *Philosophical Issues (9),* Concepts, pp. 149-162.

Hill, W. (2000). White Paper on Pharmacy: Student Professionalism. *Journal of the American Pharmaceutical Association,* 40 (1), 96-102.

Hughes, P. and More, A. J. (1997). Aboriginal ways of learning and learning styles. Paper presented at the Annual Conference of the Australian Association for Research in Education, Brisbane, December 4, 1997. Retrieved February 4, 2011 from http://www.aare.edu.au/97pap/hughp518.htm.

Jackson, R. (2009). *Never work harder than your students and other principles of good teaching.* Alexandra, Virginia: ASCD.

Jenlin, P. (Ed.), (2009). *Dewey's democracy and education revisited*. New York: Rowman and Little Education.

Jensen, E. (2008). *Brain-based learning: The new paradigm of teaching*. Thousand Oaks, CA: Corwin Press.

Johnson, D. and Johnson, R. (2009). The importance of social and emotional learning. In N. LeBlanc and N. Gallavan, (Eds.), *Affective teacher educa*tion: New York: Association of Teacher Education.

Kaplan, A. (2009). Creating democratic relationships. In P. Jenlink (Ed.), *Dewey's democracy and education revisited*. New York: Rowman and Little Education, pp. 333-359.

Kaplan EduNeering (2011). The learning is in the process not outcome. Retrieved June 27, 2011, from http://www.kaplaneduneering.com/kappnotes/index.php/2011/06/the-learning-is-in-the-process-not-outcome/

Kellough, R. and Jarolimek, J. (2008). *Teaching and learning K-8: A guide to methods and resources*. New Jersey: Person, Merrill Practice Hall.

Kincheloe, J. L. (1999) *How do we tell the workers? The socioeconomic foundations of work and vocational education*. Boulder, Colorado: Westview Press.

Kincheloe, J., Slattery, P. and Steinberg, S. (2000). *Contextualizing teaching: Introduction to education and educational foundations*. New York: Longman.

Knowles, M. (1973). *The modern practice of adult education: From pedagogy to andragogy*. Englewood Cliffs, NJ: Cambridge Adult Education.

Kurtus, R. (2001). *Being Responsible*, Retrieved from http://www.school-for-champions.com/character/responsible.htm, June 7, 2011.

Lefrancois, G. (1995). *Theories of human learning*. Pacific Grove, CA: Brooks/Cole Publishing Company.

Lekoko, R. (2009). Enriching the professional training of extension workers: Balancing skills and attitudes. *Journal of Business, Management and Training, BIAC*, 4, Issue 1I, pp. 82-94.

Lekoko, R. and Modise, O. (2010). An insight into an African perspective on lifelong learning: Towards promoting functional compensatory programs. *International Journal of Lifelong Education,* Vol. 30 (1), 5-17.

Lekoko, R. and Modise, O. (Forthcoming). Remodeling learning on an African cultural heritage of Ubuntu. A chapter to be published in In P. Jarvis and Watts, M. (Eds). *The Routledge International Handbook of Learning.* Routledge: Taylor and Francis Group. Chapter 53.

Lombardozzi, C. (2009). Breathing life into an informal learning strategy. Retrieved from http://learningjournal.wordpress. com/2009/03/29/breathing-life-into-an-informal-learning-strategy/, June 7, 2011.

Long, N. (2007). The therapeutic power of kindness. CYC_ONLINE, Issue 99. Retrieved June 10, 2011 from http://www.cyc-net.org/cyc-online/cycol-0307-long.html

Longknife, A., & Sullivan, K. (2002). *The art of styling sentences.* NY: Barron's, Hauppauge.

Mabokela, R. and Madsen, J. (2009). Leadership and democracy: Creating inclusive schools. In P. Jenlink (Ed.), *Dewey's democracy and education revisited.* New York: Rowman and Little Education, pp. 211-228.

Major, M. (2008). *The teacher's survival guide; real classroom dilemmas and practical solutions.* Maryland: Rowman and Littlefield Education.

Marks, M. A., Mathieu, J. E., & Zaccaro, S. J. (2001). A temporally based framework and taxonomy of team processes. *Academy Of Management Review,* 26(3), 356-376

Mayer, J. and Salovey, P. (1997). What is emotional intelligence? In P. Salovey and D. Sluyter (Eds.), *Emotional development and emotional intelligence: Educational implications.* New York: Basic Books, pp. 3-31.

Mbigi, L. & Maree, J. (2005). Ubuntu: The Spirit of African Transformation Management. Knowres Publishing (Pty) Ltd.

Mbiti, J. S. (1988). *African Religions and Philosophy.* London: Heinemann

McAuliffe, G. and Eriksen, K. (2002). *Teaching strategies for constructivist and developmental counselor education.* Westport, Conn: Bergin and Garvey.

Miller, J. (2006). *Educating for wisdom and compassion: Creating conditions for timeless learning.* California: Thousand Oaks.

Molesworth, M., Scullion, R. and Nixon, E. (2011). *The marketisation of higher education and the student as a consumer.* London: Routlege.

Muijs, D. and Reynolds, D. (2005). *Effective teaching: Evidence and practice.* London: Thousand Oaks.

Murithi T. (2006). African approaches to building peace and social solidarity. *African Journal on Conflict Resolution,* Vol. 6 (2), 9-34.

Naested, I, Potvin, B. and Waldron, P. (2003). *Understanding the landscape of teaching. Toronto:* Pearson.

Obinna, M. E. (1997). *Learning and teaching for continuous assessment.* New York Peter Lang.

Oblinger, D. (2006). *Learning spaces.* Washington: Boulder, CO: EDUCAUSE.

Osborne, K. (1991). *Teaching for democracy.* Montreal, Quebec: Our School/ Ourselves Education Foundation.

Patsalides, L. (2011). A definition and teacher's contemplation of lifelong learners. Retrieved February 23, 2011 from www.brighthub.com/hubfolio/laurie-patsalides/articles/38286.aspx.

Presidential Task Group September, Republic of Botswana (1997). *Long Term Vision for Botswana—Vision 2016: Towards Prosperity for All.* Gaborone: Gaborone Printers.

Ryan, N. Parcose, J. and Morse, D. (1997). Enhanced reality fieldwork: A context-aware archeological assistant. In V. Gaffney, M. van Leusen and S. Exon (Eds.), Computer application in archeology, pp. INCOMPLE

Rose-Innes, O. (2006). Sociocultural aspects of HIV/AIDS. Retrieved March 23, 2011 fromhttp://www.health24.com/medical/Condition_ centres/777-792-814-1762,23100.asp

Ross, R. (1984). Self-help groups as education. In H. Reed, and E. Loughran, E. (Eds.), *Beyond schools: Education for economic, social and personal development*. Hardley, MA: Common Wealth Company Inc., pp. 177-198.

Runco, M. (2010). Education based on parsimonious theory of creativity. In R. Beghetto and J. KaufmN, (EDS), Nurturing creativity in the classrooms. Cambridge: University Press, pp. 235-251.

Salovey, P., and Mayer, J. (1990). *Emotional intelligence. Imagination, cognition, and personality,* 9(3), 185-211.

Sanders, R. (1989). Future directions. In S. King (Ed.), *Human communication as a field of study: Selected contemporary views.* Albany, NY: State University of New York, pp. 233-241.

Santos, L. (2006). *Understanding students in transition: Trends and issues.* San Francisco: Jossey-Bass.

Sawyer, D. (1979). *Tomorrow is school.* Toronto: McClellant and Steward.

Schulle, T. Preston, J., Hammond, A. Brassett, A. and Bynner, J. (2004). *The benefits of learning: the impact of education on health, family life and social capital.* London: Routledge Falmer.

Searle, C. (1981). We are building the new school! Dairy of a teacher in Mozambique. London: Zed Press.

Semali, L. (1999). 'Community as classroom: Dilemmas of valuing African indigenous literacy in education'. *International Review of Education Journal* (45) pp. 305-319.

Silverman, M. (1996). *Active Learning: 101 Strategies to Teach Any Subject.* OH. Ally and Bacon.

Shotter, J. (1993). *Conversational realities: Constructing life through language.* London: Sage.

Shuttleworth, D. (2010). *Schooling for life: Community education and social enterprise.* Toronto: University of Toronto.

Stark, J., Lowther, M. and Hagerty, B. (1987). Responsive professional education. Washington: Association for the Study of Higher Education (ASHE, ERIC).

Stone, R. (1996). *Core Issues in Comprehensive Community-Building Initiative, Chapin Hall center for Children.* Chicago: University of Chicago

Tawney, R. (1926). Adult education in the history of the nation: Paper read at the fifth annual conference of the British Institute of Adult Education.

Tett, L. (2006). *Community education, lifelong learning and social inclusion.* Edinburgh: Dunedin Academic Press.

Tyler, F. (2007). *Developing Prosocial Communities Across Cultures.* New York:

Springer.

Vye, C., Schoojegerdes, K. and Welch, D. (2007). *Under pressure and overwhelmed: coping with anxiety in colleges.* Wesport: Praeger.

Walker, S. (2003). Active learning: Strategies to promote critical thinking skills. *Journal of Athletic Training, 38 (3), July-September 2003,* pp. 263-267.

Wang, V. and Farmer, L (2008). Adult teaching methods in China and Bloom's taxonomy. *International Journal for the Scholarly of Teaching and Learning,* Vol. 2 92), pp. (INCOMPLETE).

West, R. (1998). *Learning for life.* Final Report Review of Higher Education Financing and Policy. Canberra: AGPS.

Williams, L. (1986). *Teaching for the two-sided mind.* New York: Touchstone Books.

Zhang, L. (2007). Promoting critical thinking and information instruction in a biochemistry course. *Issues in Science and Technology, Summer, 51—www.ist/org/07-simmer/reference.html.*

WORDLIST

Botho	Means humane behavior, giving a picture of a person who is well mannered, courteous, respectful, trustworthy and disciplined (Republic of Botswana, Presidential Task Force, 1997).
Classrooms	Physical location/places usually located in school in which face-to-face (teacher-learner) learning takes place.
Community	Broadly defined to encompass all other settings outside the school environments such as the home, nation, workplaces, churches, etc.
Community skills	Capabilities, talents and abilities that learners emerge with from the learning environments that can be used to live productively with others in different settings such as homes, communities, workplaces.
Content	Is what learners learn, the subject matter with variety of sources like real life problems and challenges and theories.
Context	The location, environment including the identities, emotional state or relationships of those present in the learning environment.

Contextual deficiencies	Inability to understand the learning context leading to inappropriate learning content, ill-defined learning goals and unhealthy interactions (e.g. of learners with facilitators or with the content to be learned).
Contextual skills	Understanding the broad social, economic and cultural setting in which learning activities are taking place (Stark, Lowther and Hagerty, 1987).
Culture	Ways of life, for example, socialization process, means of survival, political activities, economic production, leadership in communities and other characteristics that bind a community together.
Emotions	Being able to have attachments to things and people outside ourselves; to love those who love and care for us, to grieve at their absence; in general, to love, to grieve, to experience longing, gratitude, and justified anger. Not having one's emotional development blighted by fear and anxiety (Coeckelbergh, undated).
Engaged learners	Learners who actively engage in learning activities both in and outside their classrooms. They take responsibility to fully interact with their learning environment through diverse strategies such discussion, acting out, dramatization, volunteering and applying what they have learned.
Facilitators	They act as guides, mentors, reflective practitioners, social activist and lifelong scholars and learners (Kincheloe, Slattery and Steinberg, 2000)
Heterogeneous learners	Learners' differences—their cultures, aspirations, ages, interest and learning styles.

Holistic learning	Learning that recognizes that to learn effectively learners' thinking, emotions, attitudes, spiritual and application have to be engaged.
Learner-centered	Learners are recognized as critical resources for learning. Learning germinates on an environment that helps learners understand themselves, their communities, families, workplace including the interpenetration of the global world and to develop skills to participate in these different settings.
Learning	A process that ingrains values or skills of how to live productively in real worlds.
Learning outcomes/ outcomes	These are knowledge, skills, attitudes, behaviors, abilities and capabilities that learners emerge with from a learning experience, usually planned one.
Learning process	The manner in which learning activities proceed or are run/handled.
Outcome-oriented learning	Both learners and facilitators are more concerned about the outcome of learning like grades or certificates than the process of acquiring these.
Practical	Engaging learners with the worlds outside their classrooms or schools to apply what they have learned and gain new knowledge and perspectives.
Process	What goes on for learning to take place, that is, the actual implementation process.
Process-oriented learning	Learning is understood more as a process of interaction in all its forms like question-and-answer, discussion, dramatization, dialogue etc. and this process is equally valued like its outcomes (grades or certificates).

Skills	Capabilities, talents, behaviors, abilities and other strategic ides that learners emerge with from a learning experience, in this case formal one.
Strategy	Synonymous with teaching-learning approach.
Thinking	Every that the conscious mind does (Fernhough, 2010).
Worlds	Different settings like homes, workplaces, churches and communities where learners are expected to apply what they learn/have learned in schools.

AUTHOR INDEX

Jensen, E.

Johnson, D.

Johnson, R.

Kaplan, A.

Kellough, R.

Kincheloe, J.

Knowles, M.

Kurtus, R.

Kurtus, R.

LeBlanc N.

Lefrancois, G.

Lekoko, R.

Lombardozzi, C.

Long, N.

Longknife, A.

Lowther, M.

Mabokela, R.

Madsen, J.)

Major, M.

Marks, M.

Mathieu, J.

Mayer, J.

Mbiti, J.

McAuliffe, G.

Miller, J.

Miller, R.

Modise, O.

Molesworth, M.

More, A.

Morse, D.

Muijs, D.

Naested, I,

Nixon, E.

Obinna, M.

Oblinger, D.

Osborne, K.

Parcose, J.

Patsalides, L.

Potvin, B.

Presidential Task Group September,
    Republic of Botswana.

Reynolds, D.

Ross-Innes, O.

Runco, M.

Ryan, N.

Salovey, P.

Sanders, R.

Santos, L.

Sawyer, D.

Schoojegerdes, K.

Scullion, R.

Searle, C.

Semali, L.

Shah, H.

Shotter, J.

Shuttleworth, D.

Silverman, M.

Slattery, P.

Stark, J.

Steinberg, S.

Stone, R.

Sullivan, L.

Takahashi, T.

Tawney, R.

Tett, L.

Vye, C.

Waldron, P.

Walker, S.

Wang, V.

Welch, D.

West, R.

Williams, L.

Zaccarosi, C.

Zhang, L.

SUBJECT INDEX

- educational
- learning
- heterogeneous
- also setting
- also environment

Cooperation and Collaboration Skills
- accommodation
- consideration
- communication
- critical thinking
- tolerance
- responsibility
- respect
- as a philosophy

Critical Thinking

Culture, also cultural
- values
- interchange sensitive

D

Debate
- as a pedagogical strategy
- as a teaching-learning strategy

Decision-making

Decisions

Dramatization
- also role play
- also act out
- also drama

E

Economic
- climate

Emotional and Relational Skills
- respect
- care
- kindness
- trust
- courteous
- disciplined
- considerate
- accommodative

- botho
- genuineness
- appreciative

Emotional Intelligence

Emotions
- undisciplined

Engaged learners
- philosophy of
- related concepts

Engagement
- active

Experiences
- real-life
- learners'
- teaching-learning
- teaching

F

Facilitator (s)
- also teachers

Family
- members
- worlds of

Field-trip
- as a learning strategy
- also field-based

Formal Learning Institutions
- also universities
- also schools

Functionality

G

Grades

Group
- work
- living skills
- also team work

Guest lecture
- also guest lecturers

H

Home visits
Homes

I

In-basket
- a pedagogical strategy
- approach
Independent
- also self-directedness
Intellectual
Interaction
- social
- learning
- directional
- physical
- intellectual
- emotional
- spiritual
- process of
Internship
- practical
- also field placement
- also field attachment
Involvement
- active

L

Learners
- engaged
- active
- lifelong
- adult
- characteristics
- as learning resources
Learning
- applied
- activities
- application of
- functional
- lifelong
- active
- contextual
- intervention
- purposeful
- field-based
- transformational
- holistic
- quality of
Lecture
- conversational
Life
- community
- way of
- challenges of
Lifelong
- learning
- scholars
Lifestyles

M

Market labor
Mentors
- also mentoring
- as a teaching-learning strategy
- also surrogate mentors
Metaphor
Model
- for engaging learners
Moral

O

Observation
Outcome
- also product of learning
- also results of learning
Outcome-Oriented Learning
- also result of learning
Outcomes
- Acquiring skills and behaviors
- outcome-oriented learning
- also results of learning
- also achievement

Surrogate Mentors
- as a teaching-learning strategy

T

Target
Teaching
- strategies
Theory/Theories
- also theoretical
Thinking
- reflective
- critical
- dialogical
- parochial
- scientific
- as a survival skill
Thinking Skills
- creative
- critical
- reflective
- analytic

- adaptive
- dialogical
- reasoning

V

Values
Voluntarism
- concept of
- as a learning strategy

W

Word-play
- puzzle as
Worlds
- of work
- of family
- global
- idealized
- future